I COWBOY

A MEMOIR

TiNille Petersen

BALBOA.PRESS
A DIVISION OF HAY HOUSE

Copyright © 2021 TiNille Petersen.

All rights reserved. No part of this book may be used or reproduced by any means, graphic, electronic, or mechanical, including photocopying, recording, taping or by any information storage retrieval system without the written permission of the author except in the case of brief quotations embodied in critical articles and reviews.

Balboa Press books may be ordered through booksellers or by contacting:

Balboa Press
A Division of Hay House
1663 Liberty Drive
Bloomington, IN 47403
www.balboapress.com
844-682-1282

Because of the dynamic nature of the Internet, any web addresses or links contained in this book may have changed since publication and may no longer be valid. The views expressed in this work are solely those of the author and do not necessarily reflect the views of the publisher, and the publisher hereby disclaims any responsibility for them.

The author of this book does not dispense medical advice or prescribe the use of any technique as a form of treatment for physical, emotional, or medical problems without the advice of a physician, either directly or indirectly. The intent of the author is only to offer information of a general nature to help you in your quest for emotional and spiritual well-being. In the event you use any of the information in this book for yourself, which is your constitutional right, the author and the publisher assume no responsibility for your actions.

Any people depicted in stock imagery provided by Getty Images are models, and such images are being used for illustrative purposes only. Certain stock imagery © Getty Images.

Print information available on the last page.

ISBN: 978-1-9822-6458-1 (sc)
ISBN: 978-1-9822-6459-8 (e)

Balboa Press rev. date: 03/02/2021

For my Parents;
You taught me about Faith

CONTENTS

PART 1

Chapter 1 1
Chapter 2 5
Chapter 3 6
Chapter 4 10
Chapter 5 13
Chapter 6 16
Chapter 7 18
Chapter 8 22
Chapter 9 25
Chapter 10 27
Chapter 11 31
Chapter 12 33
Chapter 13 39
Chapter 14 43
Chapter 15 50
Chapter 16 53
Chapter 17 56
Chapter 18 59
Chapter 19 63
Chapter 20 66

Chapter 21 70
Chapter 22 73

PART 2

Chapter 23 79
Chapter 24 82
Chapter 25 84
Chapter 26 87
Chapter 27 90
Chapter 28 93
Chapter 29 99
Chapter 30 103
Chapter 31 108
Chapter 32 110
Chapter 33 113
Chapter 34 115
Chapter 35 119

Epilogue 123
Author's Note 127
Acknowledgments 137

PART 1

"Even through life's greatest challenges,
You shall overcome."
-James W. Petersen

PROLOGUE

Jim Petersen never gave up on anything in his entire life. From his very first breath until his last; he fought the good fight with every action, word and deed. Until the moment came— as it will for most—that he declared; Enough.

Enough. Is. Enough.

Enough is when you realize that there is beauty in defeat. That failing to finish is sometimes the goal, and learning through pain was the lesson after all.

Enough is not the same as giving up. Enough is when you know without a doubt that you have to turn back. Start new. Try another path through the dark unknown forest. It is a dying of the old so a truer version of yourself can emerge.

Reaching the threshold of this precipice is daunting, we all have our limits. But—there will come a time when the yearning within overcomes fear of the unknown and you will leap into knowing, *I am Enough.*

This is our story.

On the bank of the Snake River, I sat down and wept. Through my quiet sobs, a silent prayer for help pleaded from my heart. I squinted my eyes against the sunlight glinting off the surface of the river, a dance of holy light.

A dog was barking. A high-pitched, yappy bark that mirrored the urgency I was feeling. And yet, the river's cold dark water flowed by effortlessly, rushing nowhere, unlike the walking path that led me here that was bustling with people. Young, vibrant college students with heavy backpacks. Speed walkers in matching pants and the occasional skateboarder whizzed by. It seemed as if everyone was hurrying about their day, unaware of my presence. Only my breath felt visible in the crisp air.

The Snake River slithered its way through the heart of Boise, Idaho. I had found it by accident. Not knowing the city very well, I followed the paved path that led away from St. Luke's hospital, needing a new perspective. The stuffy room, IV machine and constant beeping of the heart monitor felt like a thick blanket of misery. After finishing my shift at the bedside, I hurried along the brightly lit hallway of Floor 9, with its squeaky linoleum floor reeking of bleach, down the cramped elevator filled with worried visitors and out into the sunny, March morning.

I watched the water flow by for a long time, my thoughts a swirling mix of fear and sadness. The cold seeped through my jeans, stiffening my body to the granite rock I sat on. A heavy silence held my tears. Then, the river began to tell me a story. A tale so ancient I already knew the words.

Go with the flow, it seemed to say. *We can't stop the flow of life; it is constantly changing. Look at me! I am different with each season. Rushing and splashing by in Spring. Slow and lazy in Summer. A trickle of life left in Autumn. The Winter is the hardest; bitter cold with ice, little sunshine and no visitors. And yet, I remain. His suffering is not in vain,* the river told me. *All of you are learning many things. Pain teaches more than hurts.*

Closing my eyes, I listened to the sound of the water, a soothing familiar tune. *His suffering is not in vain,* the song of a thousand prayers; answered.

I Cowboy

The river darkened with a passing cloud and my stiff legs carried me back to St. Luke's. Speeding cars streamed by, shoppers went in and out of stores, families ate lunch at the Taco Shop. The world spun and shifted; it didn't stop. Life flowed. *Like the river,* I thought.

A rush of warm air as I entered the hospital through the revolving doors and a sanitized smell in the lobby. I stopped to let my eyes adjust. Blinking once, twice.

Once the elevator doors were closed, my shoulders relaxed. I was alone; no uncomfortable stares or half-knowing smiles, no faking happiness. I pushed the button for Floor 9, Neurology. The elevator stopped and the doors yawned open. Walking past the nurse's station, and the room with the man in a coma, his wife loyally rubbing his unresponsive feet, I rounded the corner to room 204. I opened and closed the door swiftly, not wanting to introduce the smell of the sanitized hallway into the room. His nose was very sensitive to strong smells, often inducing a headache instantly. He was sitting in bed propped up by the familiar pillows, the lights were dimmed and curtains drawn. Looking up, he smiled his half, drooping smile.

"Hi Daddy." I said and kissed his unshaven, paralyzed cheek.

"You just missed the Doctor." He answered—his voice a hoarse whisper.

"Shoot! I am sorry I was gone for so long. What did he have to say?" Looking around the room, I noticed Mom resting on the little bed in the corner with her eyes closed.

"He said I could probably go home on Friday. If, I respond well to the feedings, and antibiotics." My hand found his and squeezed gently.

I glanced up at his IV machine where the tube feed bag was hanging. It was almost empty. "Well, how do you feel so far? It looks like you are almost done with the first bag." He gave me the so-so gesture. "A little nauseous."

"They said that would happen. You'll adjust to it. And then, you can go home."

Closing his eye, he nodded in agreement.

"You look tired. Why don't you try to rest? I'll sit right here and make sure the nurses don't bother you. "He clasped my hand tightly within his and looked at me intently with his blue watery eye.

"Thank you. Thanks for being here, my Papa girl." I smiled at hearing my familiar nickname and leaned down to embrace his frail body. His shoulders, a shadow of his former frame. After readjusting the pillow supporting his neck, and fixing the oxygen tube under his nose, I settled into the chair next to him. The IV machine droned and clicked, his heart monitor beeped and my Papa slept.

2

I was three years old in the photo. I had sun kissed wavy, blonde hair and pajamas on that showed a droopy diaper. My face was smiling up at the camera with an easy smile and I was holding a large grey and white cat, its body hanging limply from my small arms. This is the photo my Dad reminisced about when I was his "Papa Girl." I never get tired of hearing how I called him Papa and was always chasing the "kiki's." I never get tired of seeing his face light up— his wide smile and bright blue eyes—now etched into memory.

3

We talked in whispers around him. His sleep was so erratic, like a newborn's. Taking shifts every 3 or 4 hours, trading nights and relieving the other at 5 am—often sneaking into the room after the short walk from the hotel we were sharing—we didn't want him to be alone, ever. If he slept for more than a few minutes at a time, his heartbeat would plummet below 40 bpm, sounding the alarm and panicking the nurses.

It had been three intense days since he was admitted into St. Luke's with double lung pneumonia. The constant deep coughing, relentless breathing treatments, heavy antibiotics and lack of sleep was visible on his face. Dark circles of fatigue began to form under his eyes, and his voice was barely a whisper now; another thing taken from him.

At first, years ago, the only sign was a little numbness under his left eye. I had tried to kiss his

I Cowboy

cheek once and he had recoiled pulling his cheek back quickly.

"Oh, don't kiss that side! Feels like a knife jolting through my face."

Mom and Dad both claimed it was from the skin cancer that had been removed from below his eye a few years back; a consequence of decades working under the sweltering sun.

"She damaged a nerve when she dug the cancer out! Those doctors just don't know what they are doing!"

This was the usual story. Growing up in an era that trained young ones to do-it-yourself and to not-trust-the-institution-of-hospitals, my Dad was not one to rush to the emergency room for anything. You had to be on the brink of death in order to get a trip to the doctor and most importantly, Dad was a Cowboy. Loose-fitting, dirt covered Wranglers, a plaid pearl-snap button-down shirt and leather vest; his uniform. He stood 6 ft 3 inches tall with a robust upper body that could wrangle a goat with one arm, and milk a cow with the other. His good looks and country boy manners won Mom's heart over at the age of 18. She was fresh out of high school when they married in the small church of their hometown. Their wedding photo makes me smile every time I look at it. They are young and vibrant with love shining from their eyes, a love that endured raising us eight kids and 48 years of marriage.

Dad was a descendant of a long line of hard-working, persevering pioneers. They were survivors and adventurers. They were ranchers and builders, well-drillers and farmers. My ancestors immigrated to America from Ireland, Scotland, England and Denmark during the mid-1800's when travel meant hardship. Months spent crossing the Atlantic on run-down ships with hundreds of others looking for a better life. Sickness and damp, dark quarters. The constant swaying and retching. Sores in their mouths that never healed. And death. It claimed them one by one. Children were wrapped in muslin cloth, prayed over and given to the sea. If you were lucky enough to survive the crossing, you still had thousands of miles more to travel by wagon train. There was no air-conditioning, iPhones or GPS. The roads were rutted, dangerous and filled with disease like cholera and small pox. Then, when they finally settled in the Utah Valley after crossing over the treacherous mountains, there were stone and sod houses to build, crops to plant and lives to start over. This is the blood that ran in our veins; a legacy handed down from strong, capable people.

The pain in his cheek became unbearable and had spread to his ear. He finally agreed to go have some tests done by the only doctor he had ever liked, who happen to be a cowboy too, Dr. Marshall.

I Cowboy

After running some basic tests, and finding out nothing, Dr. Marshall did the only sensible thing he knew to do and referred him to a specialist in Salt Lake City. Mom called me after the 4-hour round trip drive was over and they still didn't know what was wrong.

"Pray for Daddy, he is in so much pain. We are still waiting for results. I hope it's not cancer." That was almost five years ago. The specialists still didn't have an answer.

4

"I am going to Washington. I'll take the boys with me and be back in a week." Dad packed the pick-up truck with camping gear and food, loaded the three boys up and drove down the long dirt road towards the interstate. He had heard of a quaint town East of Seattle, surrounded by mountains, rivers, and lakes. Always one for an adventure, he set off in search of the fabled town. He had planned to move the family out of Utah and away from his painful past for many years. This was his opportunity to do that.

After arriving, they made camp in Tumwater Canyon, a campground just west of town. The Wenatchee River wound its way down the canyon, carving out the mountains of granite boulders on either side. They camped, fished and explored for a week. He was sold.

Within a few months, we were ready to move from the Southeastern desert of Delta, Utah to

I Cowboy

Washington; land of opportunity with emerald green trees laden with moss and freedom from a troubled past.

The day of the move, the older boys were doing important things like helping to lift boxes, couches and dressers. My job was to clean behind the refrigerator. Dust balls and clumps of hair, old dried-up food and discarded wrappers made their way into the dustpan. A song was playing on the small grey radio left on the counter. The singer's voice rang out in empty space around me. I stopped sweeping to listen closer, swaying back and forth with the beat.

After everything was loaded methodically into the back of the truck, my family of ten paused in the dusty, sagebrush lined driveway to take one last look at the single wide trailer we called home. It would be 34 years before I came back to stand in that driveway again with ghost-filled memories and a hole in my heart.

I was riding in the front of the U-Haul truck with Dad as we neared the end of the 1,000-mile journey. The rest of the family was either in the back of the moving truck or following behind us in the pick-up with Mom. The pine trees dazzled and danced in the morning light. I had never seen so many trees in my entire eight-year-old life.

"We're going to be ok, right Papa?"

"I hope so. Too late to turn back now."

He grabbed an open bag of Cheetos and tossed them to me. The neon orange crinkled bag landed in my lap. It was a rare moment to share Dad's Cheetos.

"Don't tell your Mother." He said with a wink.

The uncertainty melted as I ate the Cheetos one by one, savoring the salty treat. Thousands of trees floated by and I licked my orange covered fingers.

5

The wall heater clicked on, radiating warmth through the waiting room. I looked out at the surrounding snow-covered mountains. The sun was just beginning to peak out from the low thick clouds.

It had been a long night. Dark circles under my eyes showed my age and my short curly hair was matted and tangled. I absently ran my fingers through it in an attempt to smooth it out, then rubbed my gritty eyes. That night had been spent on a creaky twin sized bed in the corner of room 204, which barely contained my six-foot frame. Tucked in next to the window, I had spent most of the night looking up at the dark cloudless sky listening for the heart rate monitor. Once, around 3 am, the alarm on the monitor started beeping loudly. I crossed the room quickly so I could turn it off before it woke him. His head was slumped to the side and his oxygen tube had slipped out of place.

I carefully readjusted the tube under his nose and fixed the pillow behind his head. The number on the screen climbed slowly back to 49 bpm; a glow of light keeping time with his heart. Satisfied, I returned to my own bed and settled into the flat, stiff pillow. A thin white hospital blanket draped over my legs, I stared at the monitor and listened to his breathing.

I laid on my side so I could watch Dad sleep. His form across the room under the blankets seemed so small. What started out as a sore cheek had spread and grown like an unwanted virus into the whole left side of his face. Numbness, paralysis, and loss of motor function in his eye, nose, mouth and now his throat. Half of his face drooped and sagged, he felt nothing in his teeth and tongue, couldn't swallow food or water and his booming voice had been reduced to a hoarse whisper. I thought of all that had been taken from him physically, but his resilience and Cowboy character still shone from his one blue eye. Every time the nurses came into the room, he tried to joke with them about something or other. Whispering "Ha-Ha-Ha", or giving them a thumbs up. When asked how he was doing he would smile his droopy smile and whisper, "I'm wonderful." I never heard him complain. Pulling me in close for a hug that night, he had said," Don't let your life slip away, enjoy it."

Beep, beep, beep, beep. The heart monitor's constant sound and my own fear kept me from sleep. Finally, at 5am, the door opened quietly and

I Cowboy

my sister slipped into the room. Younger than me by 8 years, we had always been close. She was tall and built like me, both of us with dark blonde hair and ocean eyes. She had insisted on being here with me to help, I don't know how I could've done it without her. We were the "A-team".

"He slept pretty good. About 3 hours since the last nurse came in." I whispered.

"Oh good. Did you sleep?'

"No. I was too scared to."

"Oh no, Sis. Go back to the hotel and try to take a nap. I got it from here. You look exhausted."

"I am ok. I think I will go find some coffee and take a shower. I'll be back around ten."

"OK. Love you." She hugged me tight.

It was hard to swallow the lump forming in my throat.

"Love you too."

I had made it as far as the waiting room before collapsing onto the closest chair. Clouded eyes watching the world wake up, the sky a brilliant display of colors and my heart; cracked open, inconsolable, thrumming against my chest.

6

"*Snipes.*" *Dad whispered.*

His eyes gleamed in the twilight. I gave him a secret wink, already knowing what we are about to embark on.

After roasting hot dogs over the fire, drinking steaming cups of hot cocoa with mini marshmallows floating on top like puffy pillows and writing our names in the cool night air with a glowing firestick; this was the finale.

Camping was my family's annual vacation. Dad would tie down the canoe on top of his little red pickup, pack up the plastic grey milk crates containing food, kitchen supplies and clothes, sleeping bags for ten, an extra-large canvas army tent that smelled like mothballs and mold, the oars, the fishing poles, the wood, an axe and finally, us kids would pile in wherever there was room. Getting packed up was one giant feat and then there was picking the right campground site. Round and round we would drive looking at all the options. If Dad liked one, he would leave a child there to save the spot while circling some more just to make sure. This could go on for an hour, until he had found his perfect campsite. Now, the real fun began. Unloading, picking the right spot for the tent, pitching the tent, establishing who was sleeping where, tying the crates on the trees for cupboards, setting up the camp stove, arranging the food and where are all the sleeping bags? All hands-on deck!

"What are Snipes?" my little brother asked.

He was only six and this would be his first hunt.

"They are small hidden animals that only come out at night and are attracted to light." Dad's voice grew quiet as he explained how to catch a snipe. "The only way to catch them is to make the sound, WOOT- WOOT, and hold the flashlight inside a paper bag. You have to stay really still so it will run into the bag and then you... catch it!" He smashed the bag with his large hand. We all jumped at the sound.

"You ready?"

A rowdy bunch of kids went running in all directions making Woot! Woot! sounds; the glow of moonlight reflected diamonds on the river and Dad, crouched low behind the nearest hedge, anticipated his great scare.

"Aspiration Pneumonia." The emergency room doctor had announced to them and admitted him immediately. His coughing had become unbearable. He told us later that he remembered his own Father's demise and stubbornness with doctors, and figured it was time to give in. Mom called my little sister, Amber, who lived nearby and she rushed right over to help.

"He is severely dehydrated and malnourished. We need to start him on an IV and fluids right away." The emergency room doctor explained.

After they stabilized him, the doctor soon realized this was more than a small-town hospital could handle. He transferred him immediately by ambulance to St. Luke's in Boise, an hour away. After they arrived and Dad was admitted, it was clear they weren't leaving anytime soon.

My two other sisters and I were on our annual Girls weekend in San Diego when we got the call.

I Cowboy

The diagnosis was not good. Double lung pneumonia and a feeding tube to survive. That night, I booked our flights to Boise and we cut our trip one day short. Many small miracles later, we landed on the small runway at the Boise Airport. It was 10pm, but we drove straight to the hospital.

Dad was laden with tubes, monitors and blankets. The room was poorly lit and stale. His one open eye lit up when we entered the room and my heart dropped to the floor with my suitcase. He had lost so much weight.

"Daddy...." I choked out and hugged his sunken chest.

"Don't cry." He patted my back, comforting me. I inhaled his smell, and rubbed his scratchy cheek. A lifetime of memories held in a single scent.

"Are you going to be ok? You want us to stay here with you?" Sarah asked gently.

"No, no, no....you girls go get some rest. We're fine here." Mom said as she waved her hand around the room. Her eyes were wide with the panic only a daughter would recognize. She was always good at pretending.

A silence held our fears as we left that night. I think we all knew what was to come.

We easily found the hotel and went right to the room. Amber was already tucked in and sound asleep—I knew she was exhausted—it had been an unending loop of caring for our parents for the past few months. Unzipping my bag slowly, I felt around for my PJ's, stripped off the musky smelling clothes

I wore and slipped in to bed. The fluffy down pillow cradled my pounding head and lured me into a deep dreamless sleep.

That was days ago and it seemed as if the coughing would never stop. Every time the door opened and the Respiratory Specialist wheeled in the coughing assist machine, Dad would wince. He was complaining that his side hurt and kept pointing to his lower ribs. The intense coughing was taking its toll. I wondered if we would ever be able to hear his voice again.

The days and nights passed by in a slow march while we took turns sitting by Dad's bedside. Whatever dignity he had left fizzled out by the necessity to use the portable toilet before the nurses responded to the buzzer. "When I feel the knock-knock, there is no time to wait!" He said while raising his arms up for us to help him out of bed. I remember turning my back to let him have some sort of privacy. He didn't seem fazed by the arrangement and I did my best to hide my embarrassment.

Sarah and I let Mom have some quiet time with him while we ran across the street to a local taco shop. We felt guilty eating in front of him, knowing his future was feeding tube only. "I'd give anything for Mom's pancakes and eggs." He had said earlier that day. I tried not to think about it while we ordered food and sat down.

"Dad had a vision last night. He told me about it this morning after you left to go shower."

"Really? What did he say?"

"After finally falling asleep last night, he felt death's door open up to him. He walked through it and found himself on the other side of a very wide river. Looking back behind him, he saw all of us; his kids, his grandkids and Mom. In that moment, he knew without a doubt how much he meant to all of us. He felt like a someone. For the first time in his life, he didn't feel like a nobody..." Tears clouded her spacious blue green eyes as she reached for my hand across the white papered table. Chicken tacos and guacamole sat untouched.

"He was sent back. We still need him here."

The city of Boise grew dark with the setting sun, casting shadow and light on the surface of the Snake River; a dance between night and day.

8

Dad was the second born son to Herald and Rae Petersen. Arriving three months prematurely in 1946 didn't leave them many options. He spent the first month of his life in an incubator attached to oxygen and was fed only by a feeding tube that was placed down his throat. When he was strong enough to go home, Rae was deeply entrenched in the darkness of post-partum depression. Left at home with two babies under the age of one, she longed for her carefree days spent in Pasadena with movie stars, beaches and sun for days. Rae and her sister Pat grew up on Sunset Blvd. across from MGM studios. They would wait for hours outside to get a glimpse of anyone famous entering or leaving the building. Both of them tall and stunning; gorgeous curls, striking blue eyes and contagious laughter. Rae was a young bride, which was customary during the 40's. Soon after Dad was born, Grandpa Herald talked her into moving

I Cowboy

to his hometown of Delta, Utah; a world away from the beauty of California. Sage brush, wind, dust and rattlesnakes were her new normal.

Young mothers back in the 40's rarely breastfed their babies, so Dad was fed formula and left unattended on the bed for hours. He was barely a year old when Rae left him to go to the grocery store. While she was away, he woke up and began to roll around on the bed, wedging himself between the wall and the mattress. Crying and screaming is what Rae heard when she finally returned from shopping. She laughed when she retold me the story decades later, her stunning blue eyes an exact match to my Dad's own.

He didn't feel close to his parents. Growing up in a large family raised on a farm in rural Eastern Utah, there were chores, chores, chores. His favorite horse, Mickey, a loving companion and his brothers, Mike, Sherm, Alan, (nicknamed Smiley), and Richard; his mischievous vices. They raised Hell—and Grandpa Herald let them know it. His belt buckle and boot heels punished them when his words couldn't. Dad remembers many times witnessing his older brother, Mike, getting both.

Although he was raised to, "honor thy Father and thy Mother", Dad never felt loved. He was supposed to work, get to church, pay his tithing and mind his manners. Children weren't fawned over. They were farm hands to be seen and not heard. It's the way things were done. The damage to a young boy's self-esteem is rarely seen on the surface. Dad's sadness seeped into his body producing a massive heart-attack at the age of 56, severe digestive problems, low self-esteem, and anger. At times, he seemed to boil over with it. Just mix a traffic jam with his anger and you got an explosion!

Dad struggled his entire life to break a long vicious cycle of abuse and lack of love through his actions of raising us. He decided when we were still young that he didn't want to repeat the same mistakes his Father had. I still remember the last spanking I ever got. He hung up the brown leather belt and told us he was sorry. I know he shed tears that night with memories of his own childhood whippings. Painful pasts filled with self-loathing are healed when we can find forgiveness and self-love.

Jim; a boy, a man, my Dad, finally understood when he looked back across the wide river of his vision and realized his worth.

Grandpa Herald was raised to work and a workaholic he became. He was also the heir and sole owner of "Petersen Well Drilling," started many years before by his own Father, Joseph. He wore tan coveralls covered in grease, a tattered trucker's cap adorned his head and a welding torch; his sword. His left hand was twisted and crippled from a farm tool accident when he was 15; a handicap that never stopped him as he worked outside in the covered shop. The only time he didn't work was on Sunday.

Dad grew up going to drill sites with him and his four brothers. They knew water; how to witch it, drill for it and make it gush up to the surface from hundreds of feet below. A bubbling cauldron of fresh water soaking their pants, shoes and the red Utah dirt. A finished well job, self-employment and the wide empty desert was their calling. Although it was a family run business, Herald held the purse strings which caused friction for the boys. Through Dad's stories, I have learned two things; never mix business with family and always work for yourself.

Although the well drilling business brought in good money, it wasn't easy. Mom was constantly worried about him alone out on well jobs, working 10-12 hours a day, sometimes hundreds of miles out in the tumbleweed and dirt. Dad told us later that he turned down many jobs if it took him too far away from home even if it meant a pay cut.

He sat my younger brother down one day and questioned his work ethics. Tyler had recently graduated from Chiropractic school and had moved back home with his young family to set up his own clinic. Focused and productive, he had become a workaholic.

"What do you want your kids to remember about you, Tyler?" Dad asked.

10

"I found him sobbing on the couch one night." Mom shared with us. The occipital nerves that were responsible for motor function to his eye, mouth and cheek fired off randomly throughout the day and night. He told us it felt like sharp electrical currents shooting through his head. Any movement or small breath of air could trigger it. They tried all sorts of remedies to help with the pain. Chiropractic, massage, acupuncture, turmeric and nerve pills specially ordered from India. The list grew longer and longer and nothing seemed to work. He was refusing the prescription nerve pills from the neurologist, claiming the side effects could damage his heart even more. We knew better than to push him. Dad dug his heels in deeper when we brought up surgery.

Finally, he relented at St. Luke's. They gave him a steady dose of morphine for the pain and Gabapentin to relax the nerves. When asked about his pain level, he gave us a double thumbs up. It was numbing, sleepy, dopey headed relief.

And then there was the feeding tube. "I'd rather die than have to do that." He had said just a month before. It took hours of coercing, pictures to help explain the procedure and meeting the surgeon face to face to finally convince him. When they rolled him away on the gurney, the expression on his face made me shrivel up inside. He looked like a little boy, unsure of his fate, ready to face the unknown. As I waved goodbye to him, I couldn't help feeling like his watchful parent.

Later, when he had recovered, I cornered the nurse to ask when he could go home.

"The feedings are going well, and we might be sending him home tomorrow."

"That's great news!" I told the nurse. "When are they going to train us on how to take over the feedings at home?"

"A consultant will be here in the morning to help facilitate that." She said blankly and shuffled out the door. I was glad to see her go. Her demeanor was cold and uncaring. Whenever she walked into the room, I could see her staring at Dad's drooping face. I wanted to slap her and say, "Didn't your mother ever teach you not to stare?"

Dad was like a handsome Cowboy you'd watch on an old John Wayne movie. After he started balding in his late 30's, his hat collection grew. Eventually, he just shaved his whole head. He used to grab my long mousey blonde hair in his hand and say," Can you give me some of yours?" Before any picture was taken with him in it, he'd yell for a hat to, "Cover my bald head!"

Dad tried not to be self-conscious when his eye first started drooping. He'd wear sunglasses indoors so others wouldn't stare at it. I bought him a patch and made him try it on. That lasted all of one day. "I look like a pirate!" He laughed and took it off.

As his face started sagging more and more, he would often bite his own cheek when talking or eating. I'd look the other way when food found its home on his lip or chin, knowing he couldn't feel it. Months dragged by without a diagnosis. By the time he was sent to Boise with Pneumonia, the nerves on the entire left side of his face and neck had given up.

"I still think of you as my smiling, twinkly eyed Papa." I told him one day.

༄

"The nurse said they are sending you home soon." I told him when he woke up from a short nap. "Looks like you beat this one."

He gave me the double thumbs up, his favorite sign.

"You are a cat with nine lives."

"What number am I on?" He whispered.

I counted the near misses on my hand.

"Four." I said, shaking my head in disbelief. His life; spared one more time. "Looks like you have five more."

Another double thumbs up then he reached for his pad of paper and started writing furiously.

"I don't like Goodbyes. I like Hellos." The note said.

Have you ever had your pigeons milked? Or a horse bite on the inner thigh? How about a monkey bump? Dead leg? Rope burn on your fore arm? If you answered no to any of the above, you apparently did not know my Dad.

There were so many times I was tricked by him. Fooled into thinking that he had a very important story or joke to tell me when he'd call me over to sit by him on the couch. I was an easy target and went to snuggle up next to him thinking I was the special one that got to sit and laugh with Dad. He'd grab my hand in his, and start milking those pigeons while I squirmed and cried out in pain. Of course, this only encouraged him further. So, he'd continue with the other hand, laughing the whole time. I can still see his smile and hear his booming laughter. If I close my eyes real tight, I can still see his shining blue eyes crinkled at the corners, beaming from within. I would give anything to have those moments back. Even if it meant I had my pigeons milked over and over.

12

The walk from the hotel to St. Luke's Hospital along the main road was quiet as I made my way down the sidewalk. Tipping my chin down and stuffing my frozen fingers deeper into my coat pockets, a shiver ran down my back, the smell of woodsmoke permeated the air. Boise in March was frigid and unforgiving in the early morning. Cold weather and me did not agree. After living in California for the last 20 years and acclimating to the mild weather, these bitter cold mornings were taking a toll.

I hurried my pace while thinking of the steamy coffee waiting for me in the hospital lobby. After ordering there for several early mornings in a row, the staff was more than sympathetic. Each time I arrived, frozen and tired from another sleepless night, their eyes shone with understanding. I am sure they were used to seeing baggy eyed, worried visitors every day, but I appreciated their compassion all the same.

We had been using the hotel as our second home for over a week now. Taking shifts at the hospital and then returning for food, a soft bed or a shower. The staff at the hotel had noticed the pattern too and smiled or said hi every time we passed the front desk, sometimes stopping us to ask about Dad's condition or to see if we needed anything. Kindness shows up in the most unexpected places.

After ordering my coffee and sitting down in a nearby chair, the warm sanitized air unthawed my face and fingers. I closed my scratchy eyes and listened to the buzz of the café and quiet conversations around me, eagerly sipping hot milky coffee and thinking of Dad. He would never swallow anything ever again.

The thought grabbed at my throat, causing tears to form in the corner of my eyes. I gripped the paper cup harder trying to force the sob down. I willed myself to stop, but as coffee slid down my throat, tears slipped from my eyes. I dabbed at them with a napkin, hoping I didn't just smear the sloppy application of mascara I had put on in an attempt to look more awake.

Sleepy visitors walked by me with half-hearted smiles, approached the information desk looking for the right floor where their loved one lay waiting and wandered away—lives put on hold to be with the one they loved— sometimes for the last time. I dabbed at my eyes again, drying any remaining tears and took one last sip, emptying my cup. I squared my shoulders, took a deep breath and started the journey towards Room 204 on Floor 9.

Standing in front of the door about to enter before me was the Case Manager for Dad's hospital care. I called out to her.

"Dawn! Wait...."

She turned around at the sound of her name and gave me a wide smile. Dawn was our angel. Visits from her were like a breath of fresh air on a stuffy humid day. Anything we asked for, she made sure it happened.

"Hi, I was just about to deliver some good news."

"I love good news."

"Let's go in and tell your parents at the same time." She said as she squirted some hand sanitizer onto one hand from the dispenser outside the door. I cringed.

"Ummm, Dawn? We haven't been using the hand sanitizer. The smell gives him a headache. All the nurses wash their hands using the sink inside the room instead. Sorry..." I said hoping I didn't sound too bossy.

"Oh, that's not a problem. I'll go wash this off in the hallway bathroom and be right back!"

"Thank you, I really appreciate it." As she headed down the hallway, I quietly opened the door to the darkened room.

Mom was scrolling through her phone, and the bed was empty. She looked up as I closed the door. Pointing at the bed, I asked, "Where's Daddy?"

"He's taking a shower! We finally have a male nurse on shift and he offered to help him get cleaned up." Mom always had an optimistic spirit about her. I used to think it was naivety during my teenage years, but now, it was refreshing.

"Alright, I'll be right back. Dawn was going to come in and give us some good news, but I'll tell her to wait a few more minutes."

Mom gave me a puzzled look. "Good news about what?"

"Not sure, but she seemed happy about it... I'll be right back."

I left the room and headed down the hall in the direction that Dawn went. I had seen the bathroom down here during one of my midnight walks a few days before. I passed a small coffee and tea counter and paused to scan for some goodies. Nothing looked that interesting so I continued down the hallway looking for the bearer of good news.

After completing the entire circle of Floor 9, and not finding her anywhere, I reluctantly went back to the room hoping she hadn't beat me there. Across from Dad's room was an older man who had had a stroke. I had seen his family gathered around him for the last week, but now the door was open and the room sat empty. I thought of his sweet granddaughter and her husband that had sat by him faithfully talking and telling stories. The other day, I was standing in the hallway taking some deep breaths and she had caught my eye. Rising from her place by her Grandpa, she walked out of the room to talk to me. We exchanged our names and stories of why we were here, and then she said in the kindest way, "You look like you need a hug," and proceeded to wrap her thin arms around me with a slight squeeze and pat on the back. Her silky blonde hair smelled of strawberry soap. I thought of her now as I looked at the cold dark room, wondering what their fate had been.

Dawn was already in the room when I returned and the attending nurse was finished with Dad's shower. After eight days of lying around in a hospital gown, the hot soapy shower was just what he needed.

"Feel better, Dad?"

Double thumbs up and a half smile. "Good as new." He wrote on the notepad.

Dawn cleared her throat and began.

"So, I have some good news for you all. The VA benefits have come through and they will pay for the emergency room visit, the ambulance ride and the entire stay here at St. Luke's. They will also cover the feeding tube food and homecare nurse. We will be sending you home with an oxygen machine and suction to help facilitate the continual clearing of your lungs. This will all be covered. The only thing they won't cover is the Physical Therapist visits you will require at home. I have sent a claim into Medicare and hope to hear back within a few days. Any questions about anything? Any concerns?"

"Aww, that is such a relief! I was so worried about that claim not being accepted." Mom exclaimed. It had been nothing but an uphill battle with the VA. Mom had become a wizard at navigating the system and organizing all of Dad's appointments. Veteran's Assistance was the only medical insurance they had. After the initial search for a diagnosis started five years ago, the VA had taken care of all of his thousands of dollars in medical bills.

Mom and Dawn continued to discuss the benefits and work out the details about the insurance claims, and I sat down by Dad to help him brush his teeth while we listened. I noticed his scaly, dry white feet sticking out of the blanket. My Dad's feet were very familiar to me, yet I had never looked very close at them. I noticed his toes and snickered.

"You have webbed toes, Dad. I always wondered where I got them from."

He wiggled his feet in response.

"What do you mean? Are yours the same?"

I nodded and laughed.

My second and third toes were partially connected just like his. This was a trait that was carried throughout our family. I used to hate my toes growing up, especially after my older brother, Justin, used to tease me about them saying, "Hold her down, we'll cut them apart!"

Both of my daughters had the same toes, and a few of the other nieces and nephews. I was quick to notice his toenails too and made a mental note to get some toenail clippers and foot lotion at the nearby pharmacy. He was going to need a pedicure.

13

July 1968. Summertime in Pasadena; hot, dry and windy—where gleaming white sands hugged the rugged coastline. Crystal blue waters dotted with swaying palms and the sound of the perfect shore break was making it hard for Dad to stay in class. College in California was not for the weak minded. You needed to stay focused and stay away from the beaches!

It was his second year of classes at the Community College studying electronics. Staying with Aunt Pat and Uncle Lee was the best decision he had ever made, second to getting out of Utah. If only there weren't so many people everywhere. He was a small-town country boy that needed space. The greater LA metropolis was crawling with people, people, people. Not to mention the traffic. If it wasn't for the clear blue skies, 72 degrees every day and Uncle Lee, he wouldn't have lasted this long.

He hated electronics. The stuffy dark room packed with wires and conduit, and the professor; he was a piece of work. Dad could not understand his lectures under the thick accent that was barely a whisper. Three days a week he suffered through the class, and the other four regretted going.

That was the summer that all young men of America were being drafted. The Vietnam War was in full force and they were calling up any young man with two feet. College was the only exemption; a free pass from the War, many took that chance and put a black checkmark in the box that said, "Student."

It was a Tuesday when he discovered a white draft card in the mailbox, its black writing staring at him with its uncertainty and obligation. Sweat formed quickly on his lower back from the humidity as fear crept up his spine. He gripped the card tightly, trying to still his shaky hands. He remembers seeing Uncle Lee watching him from the wide living room window, a scowl of concern on his face.

"All you have to do is check the box for Student, and you'll be free and clear." His Uncle said confidently. They had just finished dinner, and Lee was kicked back in his favorite chair—a velour green recliner placed near the window. They often had discussions like this late into the evening, and tonight the topic was, "Draft card". Aunt Pat, (his

I Cowboy

Mother's sister), was washing up in the kitchen. Dishes clanked and pots banged with her unspoken fears. Dad knew they cared about him like their own son. He later recounted the story with tears in his eyes.

"I've decided to go."

Lee cleared his throat before speaking. "That is a dangerous decision, not to be taken lightly, you know we are at war and the Army is the first to be called up."

"I know, I know. I don't want you to worry. This decision was not made easily. My gut tells me it's the right thing to do. I have to listen, Lee. I feel it deep in my bones. This is the right choice."

Lee stared at him with teary eyes. "Then, you should go." He swiveled his green recliner away and looked out the window, his voice just a whisper. "You should go..."

ೕ

Dad was stationed at Fort Ord, near Monterey, Ca. Wide swaths of rolling hills and sand dunes dotted with Oaks, an impossible blue sky and fresh ocean breezes; the jewel of the United States Army. Every soldier trained there was headed for Vietnam, but he was happy to serving his country.

He enrolled in NCO School as soon as he could. This enabled the lowly privates to move up in rank and have more responsibility. He was promoted within a month to Drill Sergeant and was learning how to lead a troop of 15 when he got the call.

"You are going home, Jim." His Staff Sargent had said with envy in his eyes.

Grandpa Herald had injured his back while drilling a well. He couldn't work and the family business was on the brink of failure, they needed him to come home. Grandma Rae appealed to the Senator of Utah. He was honorably discharged that same week, so he packed up his small bag of belongings, put his civilian clothes back on and reluctantly went back to the dry deserts of Utah.

That same month, back in Fort Ord, the troop he was training to lead were all sent to Vietnam. Some made it back, but most did not.

Even though he was discharged, Dad still qualified for Veteran's medical benefits. At 22 years old, he could have never predicted how much that would matter.

14

We had just finished our hospital pedicure, complete with a foot and lower leg massage, each daughter assigned to a foot. Dad relaxed into the bed—but only after directing us to cut his nails straight across. Typical. His do-it-myself attitude got the better of him most of his life, but the stubborn façade was slowly melting.

"This past year has been so hard for you. Being here in the hospital with you has taught me so much, Dad." My voice dropped to a whisper. "We are all here for you."

Dad leaned back into the bed as he listened. After a few moments he gestured for me to hand him his note pad.

"Tini, thank. Love my #1 Papa girl. Go take care of yours. Thank you so much for your insights and the falcon." He scribbled.

Before leaving for the night, I tore the piece of paper off, folded it up and put it safely in my pocket. This disease seemed to be taking all his basic functions from him, I wasn't so sure I'd ever see his handwriting again.

Falcons. Signs. Hope. These all weighed heavy on my mind that night as I settled into sleep and remembered when we had seen it.

Two months before the hospital stay in Boise, I was flying on a small regional jet to visit him for his birthday. The flight was bumpy as I sat looking out the tiny window at circles and squares. Miles and miles of brown and yellow farm land dotted with little towns, rain clouds gathering above them. Flying was not my favorite, especially alone. My hands gripped the arm rests as my jaw tightened with each dip of the wing or drop in altitude. Small, shallow breaths escaped my mouth. Finally, we started the descent. I wiped the sweat from my face, lengthened my breath and steeled my thoughts on Dad. The book I was reading lay on my lap. I opened it and read through the discomfort attempting to distract myself. The author seemed to be talking directly to me. "Sometimes we find ourselves lost and afraid in life. We have forgotten about the

I Cowboy

unseen miracles and guides that are helping us at all times. Ask for a sign that everything is ok and that you are on your right path. Ask for a sign."

I closed the book and my eyes as the plane got closer to the ground. Ask for a sign. The words repeated over and over in my head as the landing gear touched land and my body relaxed with a sigh.

It was much worse than I thought. He had lost so much weight and strength. He sat in his recliner most of the day watching movies. He felt dizzy and weak just trying to walk to the bathroom down the hall and his lanky strong legs were swimming inside the grey sweats he wore. Justin had sent him a walker and a wheelchair to help, but every time he stood, I jumped up to be right beside him, making sure he didn't fall. Mom never left him alone.

"I feel bad eating in front of him." Mom told me quietly as she blended up a protein shake for him. Dad's mouth was so numb he was having a hard time chewing. He couldn't swallow water or he would cough and choke for several minutes and the yogurt he tried to eat came back up after several attempts to swallow it. Blended, soft foods and juice were his only sustenance. His body was shrinking day by day. I searched the internet for advice.

"I think we need to thicken his water, so he can swallow it. This website I was looking at has some thickening powder that is flavorless." I reported to Mom the next morning. "He needs to drink water or he will get dehydrated. Maybe that is why he feels dizzy all the time."

Mom looked thinner too. Her raggedness carefully hidden beneath clean clothes and makeup, but the undereye concealer couldn't hide her worry. I could see her fatigue in the way she walked across the room.

"I don't think he will drink it. You know how stubborn he is."

"I am afraid we don't have a choice. I'll talk to him about it, maybe he will listen to me."

Her small sad smile broke me.

That night, as I lay down to sleep the heartache away, I asked the angels and guides for some kind of sign that he would get through this. Send me a falcon, I whispered in the dark. A falcon. Please send a falcon. Faith over fear the book had said. Faith over Fear.

I woke up to sun and blue skies shining through the lace covered windows of the little quaint cottage I had rented. I wiped the sleep out of my eyes, my mouth yawning wide. Reaching beside me for my phone on the bedside table, I texted Mom to see if she was awake.

- *Good morning! It's a beautiful day. Let's take Dad for a drive.*
- *Ok! I'll ask him if he's up for it. He had a bad night.* She wrote back.

I Cow

- *I'm getting ready and will be over in an hour. Need anything?*
- *No, we are fine. See you soon.*

I sunk back into the mattress and brought the thick blankets back up to my chin. Soft morning light shone through the window lulling me back into dreamland. The room was chilly—the bed a rich haven of sleep—I did not resist.

The dream was short; a flash of pictures, images from the past, warmth and light. I awoke with a jump like I'd been shaken. I hung onto the dream by a thread, keeping the image behind my eyes, willing it to the surface. It was a falcon. In full flight.

Later, when we had packed the front seat with pillows for support and walked Dad down the sidewalk, his hands gripping the walker, an icy chill in the air, and headed out of town towards the hills, I wondered if this was a good idea after all. Dad's hands were shaky as he buckled himself in. The short walk from the front door to the car had wiped him out.

I turned off the main road and took a back road, (Dad loved the back roads), so we could inspect the nearby farms up close. The narrow winding road was lined with fresh snow, sunlight glinting off the surface. Every time we passed a big farm, fenced and plowed, waiting for the spring thaw, Dad would comment, "Good for them. What a nice-looking piece of land."

As we rounded a corner and headed down a small hill, there it was; outstretched wings painted with brown and black, small beady eyes looking for prey, soaring on the wind, sun on its back. A falcon.

"Look! Look at that bird! It's a falcon." I practically shouted.

"Oh! Yes, there it goes." Dad pointed as it glided in front of our car and down the hill, disappearing into the trees.

"Where? I don't see it." Mom said half-heartedly from the back seat.

"Over there, Myrna. There it goes into the trees."

"I've never seen a falcon before." She commented unknowingly.

The rest of the drive became a blur. All I could think about was the falcon. It surely was the sign I had asked for, wasn't it? I know I didn't imagine it. Both my parents saw it too.

I left the next day. Dad insisted they go to the airport with me, a one-hour drive away. Earlier that morning I took pen to paper and wrote him a letter. The words came easily as I told him how I felt. I wanted him to fight. I reminded him of his strength and how much he meant to all of us. I told him about the falcon; the sign that all would be ok, a message of hope, a message of help from unseen places. When he hugged me goodbye at the airport, I slipped the folded-up letter into his hand saying, "This is for you, Papa."

I Cowboy

They drove away, waving from the window. Helpless sadness sunk deep within my chest as I watched them disappear down the ramp and into traffic. I wheeled my luggage to the nearest bench and sat down. Tears streamed freely down my cheeks and travelers going to faraway places zigzagged their way around me, never knowing the burden I carried within.

After that day, I looked for falcons everywhere. A secret message from unseen places, they appeared to me at random. I seldom miss one, now. Their calls from the wild will my eyes heavenward; an angel's disguise.

15

The white house sat at the top of the hill. Peeling paint and untouched weeds, a path grown over with unkempt bushes. We walked by it every day on our way to school, the park, the grocery store for donuts, or the pool. The old man who lived within its walls was rumored to be a hermit; grouchy and untouchable. Once, I had seen him peeking out from the front door, a forlorn pitiful look across his face. Of course, I looked away, it was bad luck to see him. Nobody knew who he really was, and nobody cared.

The sun shone fiercely that day, baking the street and my neck. Squinting my eyes against the glare, I held tight to Dad's calloused hand as we marched up the hill. He snatched me from the front yard chores of pulling dandelions and said we had an errand to do. I was happy to go and leave the dandelions behind. Thinking we were on a secret mission to the grocery store I headed towards his red pickup truck parked in the driveway.

I Cowboy

"No, we're walking. This way." He said and pointed towards the street.

Baffled, I followed him, down the driveway and up Whitman street. The hill was steep and I had to run trying to keep up with Dad's pace. The sweat dripped down my back and puddled at my waistband. A sweet sickly smell reeked from my armpits.

"Where are we going?" I dared to ask.

"To meet a neighbor."

As we neared the top of the hill and turned left towards the hermit's house, I crinkled my nose in disgust, "In there?" I looked up at Dad's face with all the courage my twelve-year-old face could muster.

His answer was to reach for the gate and unlatch it pulling me into the forsaken yard along with him. He half dragged me up the weed covered sidewalk to the steps. Squaring his shoulders and clearing his throat, he dropped my hand and approached the door alone.

Knock, knock, knock. His knuckles rapped on the worn wood door. Inhaling, I waited. Exhaling, I waited. A stooped over forgotten man slowly opened the door. His eyes raked over the balding 6-foot 3-inch man on his doorstep and a wide-eyed frightened girl standing behind him. He didn't talk. Just stared. Time slowed down. Finally, Dad spoke.

"Hi, my name is Jim Petersen, and this is my daughter, TiNille." He said and waved his hand in my direction. I half smiled—half winced at hearing

my name. Why did he have to tell him my name? I wondered. "We live just down the road. I just wanted to introduce myself and to check and see if you needed anything."

I stood there in the blistering sun listening to them chat. I kicked a toe at the weeds, and shuffled from one foot to the other. Even my feet were sweating, making my feet slide inside my new jelly sandals.

The man lived alone, and had a disability. Dad offered to come help out in the yard. I couldn't believe what I was hearing and watched in disbelief as they shook hands and exchanged phone numbers. The grouchy man smiled as we waved good-bye. Dad put his hand on my shoulder as we closed the gate behind us, the weight of that moment sinking into the muscle there. Dad whistled the whole walk home.

16

Sarah was scheduled to fly out in just a few hours. I was staying one more day. It had been nine long days here in Boise and I was so relieved to be going home. My own family missed me and it dawned on me as I sat in the plastic chair next to Dad's bed, holding his hand; we were parenting our parent.

We spent the day by Dad's side and had to force Mom to go take a break. She was forgetting to eat, take restroom breaks and breathe. Her hands shook when she texted on her phone. Fatigue was like that. It crept up slowly without notice and then one day you look in the mirror and see the dark circles, the limp hair, the grey pallor. Mostly, it was denial. She was facing the unknown and it would be another long night for her sleeping in the too small bed. Thankfully, our reprieve, (3rd youngest sister, Amber) would be here only hours after I left to take over and help them get back to their home in Weiser, an hour's drive away. They lived a few short blocks from her so she could check on them regularly. The house used to be a Chiropractic office that the eldest, Justin, had owned and converted into a home for them.

Looking back now, getting them to move into the house, and out of the RV they were living and travelling in, had been nothing short of a miracle. For two years they lived like nomads. It had always been their dream—the road, freedom and adventure—then, Dad began to decline. His eye drooped so much he was having trouble seeing clearly. The pain settled into his head and cheek and kept them grounded for days. Then weeks. Months went by and they hadn't driven the RV anywhere. That's when Justin convinced them to move into the home in Weiser. A son's abiding love for his parents and authentic generosity; an inexorable force of goodness.

The doctors were confident he would be ready to go home by Friday but we were all uneasy about the home care and the feeding tube. It would be a full-time job for Mom, caregiving often is. Amber had agreed to drive them home and get them set up and two more siblings, Jan'l and Kade, would arrive the next day and stay for a week or two. A blessing of having a large family, there was always someone to help.

I Cowboy

As the afternoon light shifted towards the surrounding mountains, and the clock ticked towards Sarah's departure, the time felt right. We sat by Dad and filled the room with our shaky, tear filled song. We started with the first tune he sang as a child. It was his favorite.

His sunken face and drooping lips mouthed the song as we sang. He knew every word. The room was filled with light; a softening of our souls connecting in ways that I had often missed growing up. I had never felt so close to him in all my life.

Our relationship had been strained for several years after I pulled away from and left the religion I was born into. Always labeled the rebellious one, I was just like him in so many ways. Our tendencies to be curious and question life and its rules; we didn't like being told what to do. Dad was the only one who understood me, and tried to guide me back to their way of life several times. It was not to be. I found my own way. But, every choice in life has its own consequences. The closeness I felt as a child to my Papa would be buried for many years; like a forgotten hatchet underneath a wood pile. Until now.

17

Cigarette smoke curled around my face, stinging my vision, so I closed my eyes and pursed my lips, inhaling a long drag of nicotine. The radio could be heard faintly through the closed front door. Spring night air mixed with laughter, the smell of beer and cigarette smoke and a warm glow from the streetlamp all made me feel dizzy. I leaned into the wooden porch rail behind me and tried to focus on my friends' faces.

We had pulled it off. My parents had no clue where I was and I couldn't be happier. Jess and Scott were laughing about something and then stopped, a look of surprise in their eyes. I glanced over my shoulder and saw what they were staring at.

"It's your Dad!" Jess exclaimed in horror.

The little red pickup truck was making its way down the empty street. Blinding headlights searching in the dark, slowly inching toward us.

I Cowboy

There was the sound of shoes scuffling on the porch, bodies hurling and diving into the bushes, and the low hum of the engine getting closer. I was left standing alone and contemplated jumping over the rail too. Someone coughed. I dropped my lit cigarette on the porch and quickly stomped it out. The truck's headlights; a spotlight on my lonely predicament. Standing there, I knew my façade was up. I couldn't lie my way out of this one.

The driver side window rolled down and Dad's angry face looked back at me.

"Get in." He grumbled.

I walked down the porch stairs slowly and cast a mournful glance behind my shoulder. My lonely footsteps echoed loudly in the starless night and the street lamp cast a shadow over me. I knew my friends were watching from their hidden place within the bushes. I longed to be hidden too.

I climbed into the truck, sitting behind Mom in the small fold out jump seat.

Dad didn't waste any time.

"So, you're smoking now?"

"You're in a lot of trouble, young lady." Mom added.

I stayed silent the rest of the drive home while they exchanged glances back and forth several times as if speaking a secret language.

The verdict; I am grounded for the entire summer. I tried not to cry. The entire summer! I would miss out on so much. I tried not to sound whiny when I asked him when I could see my friends again.

"When you see Christ's light shining from your eyes."

After they had gone to bed, I locked myself in the bathroom and turned on the light. Bringing my face within inches of the mirror, I stared into my own hazel eyes. The light of Christ. It was in there somewhere, I thought. After lecturing me for hours about friends and bad choices, I felt raw and undeserving. I stared and stared. What I saw; a confused, rebellious teenager with four new pimples forming on her chin and a craving for acceptance so deep inside it scared me. I never did ask him how he found me that night. I guess a Father always knows.

18

Sarah left for the airport in a flurry of tears. It left a hole in all of our hearts. After walking her to the hotel to retrieve her bags, and putting her into the taxi for the airport, I went back to the hospital to say goodnight to Mom and Dad.

The room felt empty and void of light. Mom had pulled the shades down on the window, and was sitting next to Dad holding his hand. She looked concerned.

"Don't worry, Mom. Sarah is on her way to the airport right now. She'll be fine."

"She seemed so emotional when she left. I am worried about her."

"I helped her calmed down and she is safe in a taxi right now. Nothing to worry about." Mom was always worrying about one of her eight children, which was understandable given the responsibility she must have felt—the daunting task of raising children, supporting each one of them through all life's foibles and then setting them free to become their own person. She was still holding on to Sarah with tiny bits of thread; the last born still trying to leave the nest.

I hugged her tight. She was on the verge of a breakdown. I could sense it. This week had put us through a wringer, several times. We all had baggy eyes and broken bodies. Sarah and I got to go home and resume our somewhat normal lives after this. Mom and Dad could not escape. They had a marathon to run and this week was just the first mile. I wondered if we would ever find an answer or a diagnosis. And if we did, would it matter? What if they told us it was incurable? Then what?

All of this was weighing on me that night as I made my way back to the hotel. The air stung my cheeks, forcing me to tuck my chin into my thin coat. I picked up my pace and focused on the sidewalk in front of me. As I neared the warmly lit doors to the lobby, the phone in my pocket vibrated, alerting me of a text message. It was from Sarah.

- *I just landed, Sis. All ok there?*

Relieved to hear she had made it safely back to Portland, I replied immediately.

- *Good news! Safe drive home, and get some sleep!*

- *Mom and Dad ok?*

I Cowboy

- *Yes, they are fine! I tucked them in and at the hotel right now.*

- *Love you Sis, so glad we were together. The A-team!*

Couldn't have made it through the week without you.

- *The A-team! It was a hard week for sure.*

- *So happy you were with me. Sleep well tonight. I'll call you tomorrow.*

I walked into the warmth of the lobby and headed straight for my room on the second floor. The soft bed and empty room were calling to me. I couldn't wait to sink in and sleep a few hours. My plan was to get back to the hospital by 6 am so Mom could have some time for herself in the morning. It was my last day in Boise and I wanted to spend it by Dad's side.

Somewhere, far away on the other side of Grief and Longing, there is a place filled with Hope. Where Sadness disappears and is replaced with Joy. Where Fear is transformed into an unshakable Faith. A place where a soul can remember why it's even here. A place where Love is the only answer and Peace prevails. This place is called Never Never land. The ancient mystics and prophets wrote books and taught thousands of people how to get there. You have to sit down, be still and quiet your mind.

Stop thinking and end all your problems, they said. I believed it could be done, but that night as I lay down in bed and closed my eyes, a whirlwind of thoughts and fear sweeping through my mind, the only way to Never Never land; precious sleep.

19

A white single wide trailer sat parked on a small parchment of land in Southeastern Utah. Surrounded by sage brush, old bikes and toys. My family moved here from Nevada; where the backyard was a dry open desert and rattlesnakes slithered under rocks where we played. Here, the sun baked our skin a warm brown and dust settled daintily on everything we owned. Wind and weather shriveled the earth into dry mud flakes and our skin—no lotion could ever compete. I was nine years old and exploding with joy. A new baby was on its way.

There were nine of us in the small trailer. With three small bedrooms, we were all required to share a room. Dad built a special bed to accommodate the girls' room. A triple bunk bed, and I got the middle. I loved climbing up into my bed and wrapping myself up in my purple quilted blanket. I woke up each day to the sound of my sisters rolling around above and below me. We barely had enough room to sit on the *floor and play, so we spent most of our time outside riding bikes or building forts. The boys were down the hall and had a small walkway between their bunk beds. Four boys crammed into one tiny room; socks and underwear strewn about, stink and dirt permeating the air.*

The girls were hoping for another sister. I crossed my fingers and prayed and prayed for Mom's baby to be a girl. Dad was sure of it. He had dreamt about her.

"Seven children are enough!" Mom told him over and over. "I don't want another baby!"

Dad told her about the vision he had. He had dreamt of a little girl with blonde hair that was waiting to come to our family. Mom was not convinced. After her last birth, which they decided to have at home, she was putting her foot down. No more kids! It took a miracle to change her mind. It happened when they moved us to Utah.

The road they were driving was steep and winding in the old borrowed trucks packed with kids and furniture; a sweltering cloudless day, heat rising from the road. Dad was driving his Father's orange pickup truck and Mom followed close behind. Dad's truck stopped abruptly in the road. Panicked and confused, Mom jumped out to see what was wrong. The engine had quit. Dad cursed and steamed, opened the hood and went to work. He was always fixing something, so Mom didn't worry at first. After an hour, she panicked. She had seven kids and their whole lives parked on the side of a hill in the desert. No phone, little water, and no fellow travelers to ask for help.

"Surely there will be someone soon!"

"Myrna, there is no one coming to rescue us. We have to figure this out."

"The kids are getting hungry, Jim."

"They won't starve. Just let me look at it one more time."

Dad stuck his head under the hood for the hundredth time and fiddled with this and that. We had grown bored of waiting and complaining, and took sporadic naps while our empty stomachs rumbled. It had been two hours since the breakdown and Mom started praying and begging for help. Her one condition; get this dang truck started and I'll agree to have one more baby!

Dad peeked his head out from under the truck, forehead dripping with sweat, his face red with anger and yelled, "Try to start it now, Mimi." She sat down in the front seat, gripped the wheel and turned the key. We all held our breath as the truck roared with life. Dad jumped up and down pumping his fists. Relief flooded the dry stale air and cleared the panic like a summer rain. They hugged and laughed for the first time that day, then drove us the hell out of there.

A year later; a baby girl with a whisper of blonde hair was born into the Petersen Tribe. They named her Sarah.

20

At first light on the third Friday in March, the lungs of Jim Petersen were finally starting to clear. After spending nine days rooted to his side like an old tree in the earth, Mom was anxious to get him home. I pulled the attending physician into the hall so I could drill him with questions.

"What happens now?"

"We will continue to monitor his lungs and make sure the infection is clear."

"Then he can go home?"

"Well... at that point we will have someone here to help guide you in the process of feeding's at home and getting you set up with a consultant."

"Your Dad will have to continue on the tube feedings. His respiratory specialist has given orders for no food or water by mouth. We will send a Home nurse aid to come visit him and re-evaluate his airways twice a week. I've also ordered in-home physical therapy and a consultant to be on-call if you need any guidance with the tube feedings."

The doctors' sandy blonde hair and young eyes softened his abrasive demeanor. I cleared my throat and squared my shoulders.

"My Dad has been searching for answers for five years. He has been mis-diagnosed over and over and I really want to push for him to get more testing. Who is the best neurologist or specialist that you can refer him to?" My voice sounded unfamiliar to me, high pitched and desperate. Sweat started forming under my heavy sweater.

"We are working on getting an authorization for him to see a specialist in Portland at OSU. They have multiple neurologists there who study rare cases like this all day long. It's his best bet."

I inhaled deeply trying to process what he was saying. I tried not to shout. "Nothing we have done has worked so far. Nothing. What makes you so sure that they will figure it out?"

A sadness spread over his face and clouded his eyes. "I'm not sure. We can never be sure when it comes to the nervous system. Researchers all over the world are still discovering new diseases all the time. A hundred years ago, we didn't know what Parkinson's disease was. So far, no one has diagnosed your dad incorrectly. His symptoms have all matched several other diseases. What makes his so unique is what we need to figure out. Like I said, it's his best bet. Take the first appointment they have."

We shook hands and he turned to leave. I stood there for several minutes transfixed; his worn brown loafers on the white linoleum floor kept perfect time with his next appointment. With a forced smile on my face, I went back into the darkened room of 204.

"I Cowboy" was Dad's life motto; a shortened version of, "I am a Cowboy!" These words defined him. It was his core reason for carrying on; mucking through obstacles and horse stalls, paying bills and switching jobs, finding ways to feed his growing family. The only problem; cowboys don't trust doctors. They trust home remedies, Epsom salts, and colloidal silver. He raised us to think like him. Growing up, we rarely went to see a doctor. So, it was no wonder the nurses cringed whenever I approached their station at the end of the hallway, their faces pinched and ready for my demands. Dad called me his "Go-to-Girl" and told me he liked how I took charge. Too bad the nurses didn't agree. Bracing for his reaction, I told him what the doctor had said.

"Dr. Whitely wants you to see another specialist in Portland."

He tried to furrow his brow, but only half of his face responded. The cues from his brain frozen within unmovable cells.

I Cowboy

"No more tests." He wrote on the pad of paper he kept nearby.

"There will be no more tests, Dad. They will send all your medical records ahead of your appointment and hopefully be able to see some sort of pattern. I think this is your only chance of getting any sort of diagnosis. It'll be ok, I promise." The river's wise words resounded in my mind. I had to tell him. "Dad, your suffering is not in vain," I said softly. "You're teaching us so much. Remember what you told me all those years ago?"

The day is sealed with this; stars whirled on their endless journey across time, and a sheaf of golden light seeped its way into the discouraged heart of a Cowboy I called Papa.

21

I was late again. It was well past midnight and I knew Mom would be furious. Thinking I could sneak into the house without her hearing me was wishful thinking. She was waiting by the front door. I hung my head, not wanting to look her in the eye.

"Your Dad wants to see you." She said and went directly to her room.

I sighed deeply and put my shoes back on, shut the heavy wood front door behind me and started down the porch stairs. The night was cool on my skin and the light from the streetlamp cast eerie orange shadows on the street. I took the path across from our house, cutting between the neighbors adjoining yards and entered the park behind them. Grabbing the metal merry-go-round with my hand, I shoved it with all my strength and watched it spin; round and round it travelled—a scent of metal wafted past my nose reminding me of a girl that used to enjoy this ride—a simpler time.

I Cowboy

I sat on the swings and held onto the cold thick chains to steady myself and leaned back to lift my legs high. My long curly hair fanned out beneath me brushing the dirt below. I looked up at the sky and rehearsed my excuse for being late. Swinging back and forth, I slowly built up some courage.

The Hotel was across a wide parking lot next to the park and the community pool. Both my parents worked there, which was convenient for everyone. Mom worked during the day, and Dad filled in the Night Auditor shifts a few times a week. My sister and I both worked in the breakfast room—famous for their omelets—on the weekends and sometimes for housekeeping. The Hotel was a family run business so the owners enjoyed having our family work there too. Dad was working all night and I knew he was waiting for me.

I approached the brightly lit lobby with the wide hand carved double doors. I could see him at the ornate front desk through the windows. His head was bent down as he shuffled through a stack of papers. Here goes nothing, I said to myself and opened the doors to the lobby. Warm air rushed out to meet me with the faint sound of music playing from the radio. A scent of freshly brewed coffee tickled my nose.

He looked up and our eyes met. He didn't smile, just lifted his hand and beckoned me over to the desk. I crossed the carpeted room and stood facing him. The desk separating us; an obstacle of unspoken misunderstandings between a father and daughter.

"Hi, Dad." I finally said.

"You worried your Mother again." He grumbled without looking up.

"I know. I'm sorry to be late again. The ride I was getting home took longer than I thought it would. Next time, I promise not to be late." My voice didn't sound sincere so I scrambled to make up for it. "I really promise, Dad."

He didn't speak for an eternity, but continued to separate the pile of paper in front of him into two piles. The noisy printer next to him was spitting out copy after copy after copy. I wondered how long I would have to stand there and glanced up at the cuckoo clock hanging on the wall. Hand carved and imported from Germany, the hands clicked dutifully towards 2 am. I shuffled my impatient feet from side to side.

Finally, after all the papers had been sorted through and my legs ached from standing still, he looked up. His eyes gleamed with a knowingness that only a parent could know—a sureness of the struggles to come and wisdom from life's inevitable lessons—and said, "Your life is not your own, TiNille."

22

Sunlight streamed through the crack in the drapes covering the large window. The beams of light landed softly on my face, waking me from a dreamless sleep. I yawned and stretched my arms upwards, working out my forty-two-year-old kinks. I was going home. Bags needed to be packed, words needed to be said, time must be spent by Dad's side.

The walk to the hospital was frigid as always, but I found myself not minding it knowing Dad was going home the next day. He beat pneumonia, a rare feat for someone his age and in his condition. My Cowboy Daddy was stronger than anyone could know; fearless, determined, humble.

The day crept by like all the others before it, but this time I paid attention; to his face, his hands and bald head. I sat and talked for hours about his home care, his life, his strength. I wanted to soak up as much of him as I could, mostly out of love, but partly out of fear. After I left later that day, I wasn't sure when I would see him again; my heart ached with the thought.

My sister, Amber, and her son, Peter, were arriving later that day to take my place. We were all worried about Mom—although she was happy to have Dad be released, she was also timid and unsure how life at home would look under these very hard circumstances. We talked while we waited for the home care nurse to arrive for the tutorial. Different scenarios would require them to have more help, and I tossed the idea around that they might need to either move in with one of us, or hire a full-time nurse. After discussing all the options available to them, we came up with a plan. A very rough plan, wrote out on scrap paper, signed by both of them, and sent to all the siblings—because as Dad said, "There were many Chiefs and no Indians."

The sun tracked low in the cold March sky and the clock ticked the hour of my departure. It was time. I gathered my strength, hugged and kissed them both, wiped away tears, and left for the airport. My body wracked with fatigue, my heart broken open, and the love for my parents; immense, unhidden, pure.

I sobbed the whole flight home.

PART 2

One year later

"A little stretching always takes place
for growth to happen for all of us."
-James W. Petersen

*"Remember me in the family tree;
my name, my days, my strife.
Then I'll ride upon the wings of
time and live an endless life."*
-Linda Goetsch

23

The fierce desert wind shook the car and blasted me into the next lane. I gripped the wheel and forced myself to breathe. *Stay calm, you are in control*, I thought to myself. Dad's words echoed in my mind. *Get into the next lane and slow down. It'll be ok.* I felt held by his presence as my eyes focused on the lane lines like an eagle swooping in for prey. After endless miles of wide-open country dotted with sage and cactus, the sun baked earth gave way to sandstone cliffs painted red. My solo road trip was at its end. Seven hundred miles from California to Utah; I swore I'd never come back here, but life will have its way with you.

It has been a year. An incomprehensible, grief-stricken year. Most of it was spent in a wide-eyed fog. The eyes are open and you are moving, but your spirit has been trampled, washed up, wrung out. The body knows how to move one foot in front of the other, one task at a time for days and weeks and months on end. It's the heart that stays still. Unmoving, frozen in grief. Afraid. The heart stays heavy with unspoken words and unshed tears—it thrums and beats to the drum of life, refusing to let the claws of grief dig in. My shattered self, hid deep within a cocoon. What emerged after a year of mourning was an unshakeable trust in life. A butterfly unfurling its wings for the first time, following instinct only, trusting that this new life will still be beautiful.

The Oasis Cemetery sat alone in the desert, lined with Birch and Pine trees, and perfectly manicured green sod swaying gently in the breeze. It held the memory of my Papa's funeral; a rain soaked, shivering crowd, heads bowed, eyes red and swollen. "Taps" played by a solo trumpet, a six-gun salute which startled the falcons that flew from the trees. They circled us and landed with ease in a nearby Birch. There was an American flag lifted from the casket, folded methodically and solemnly handed to Mom. She clutched it tight to her chest as we laid deep red roses on top of the Pine casket, and the hole gaping open that swallowed him; a yawning abyss of earth that would never let him go. The Oasis Cemetery held the Cowboy whose absence would rock all of our lives.

I drove seven hundred miles to stand with my family at his graveside and honor him one year

I Cowboy

after he passed; I felt his essence with me the entire way. He always loved a good road trip. A badly folded map would sit resting on his lap, along with oatmeal cookies or Cheetos, dark aviator glasses adorning his face, and the thrill of finding new places; his compass. I reached for my own bag of Cheetos and licked the orange coating off my fingers. I breathed a sigh of relief knowing I was near the end of the year long journey; to a place of acceptance.

24

Two weeks passed in a blur of tubes, pills and feedings. Dad's schedule was a rigorous one and it took many attempts before they mastered it. Written down on a white board—in red, blue and black ink—food, pill and water schedule for the day broken down into times and amounts. 120 ml food, followed by 60ml water, followed by crushed up painkillers mixed with water, repeat, repeat, repeat. If he was discouraged, he never let on. The unspoken fears of this new reality only slight whispers on their lips.

It was early April when they got the call that changed everything. It was Portland's Research Department at Oregon State University. They had an appointment available the next day. Portland was a four-hour drive with good weather and no stops. Dad would need to be fed every two hours and there was a rain storm on the way. Despite the challenge ahead of them, they planned to leave as soon as possible.

It was a whirlwind of packing, planning and preparing for the next few hours. Finally, at 4 pm, they were on their way to Portland with their hearts pushing up against their chests.

The cars pulled out of the driveway, and headed west towards Oregon. The fog was so thick it made it hard to see the road.

As they waved goodbye to Amber and her kids, with tear-stained faces and uncertainty weighing heavily in the air, a gentle wind signaled the arrival of rain. "It will all work out." Dad whispered and gave his signature sign. Double thumbs-up, and a nod of his head.

25

We met in Oasis Cemetery at eleven in the morning. Five of the eight kids were present and a scattering of grandkids. Forming a circle of chairs around his headstone, we sat still, our hushed voices; a melody on the wind. After a while, Mom played music and talked of love, sacrifice, family, and gratitude. She brought red roses for everyone to place in the vases cradling each side of the stone. Mature Birch and Pine trees encircled us; their mighty branches like arms from Mother Earth. Tears of laughter, tears of grief. Stories told and retold. Memories shared of Dad's wisdom, his love, his legacy. Sunshine spilled down from the heavens upon our broken hearts. *Life is unending and flows on and on,* it seemed to say.

Afterwards; we gathered for a family photo and shouted in unison, "I Cowboy!" As the camera frame froze that moment in time, I thought of Dad resting in the earth below us and his children carrying on, still here, walking upon it. We are his legacy, I thought. He was right; *our lives are not our own.*

I was twelve when Dad brought home the firetruck red Coleman canoe. He pulled into the driveway with it strapped to the top of his pickup truck, a wide grin on his face. We used that canoe every time we went camping, it was part of the family. It held our stories within its curved sides and well-worn oars. Many times, we had tipped over, dumping us and all the contents into a cold lake. There was a time that Dad tipped us on purpose just to see what we would do; swim to shore or try to climb back in. When all eight of us had moved out and had our own families, he gave it to younger brother, Tyler, who had seven kids of his own.

That day, it was decided we would honor Dad by taking the red canoe out to the Delta Reservoir. A place where Mom was wooed and courted by Dad on many sweltering hot nights when she was still in high school and falling in love.

We arrived at the Rez in a cloud of dust—five cars and thirty people, towels, chairs, coolers, pop up tents—unloaded and set-up in under ten minutes. Bags of chips torn open, kids shouting, dogs barking. This was the chaos I knew and loved. Then, Tyler's white ten passenger van pulled into the parking lot, full of kids and laughter, a red canoe strapped to the top. Like Father, like Son.

In my mind's eye I could see the shape of my Dad helping unstrap the canoe from the tie-downs, lift it up over his head and walk towards the water. His tall frame and strong arms easily flipping the canoe over and placing it in the water, beckoning to us to get in. His sparkling blue eyes would shimmer with mischief as he pushed us off the shore and into the water's depths, saying, "Get those oars going now, easy, easy, don't tip." All the while his hands would pull one edge down and then the other, making the boat rock slightly. "Dad!!" We would all cry out, making him snicker.

A simple red canoe; time capsule, magic maker, a link to our past. Now, in the water once more with me in front and Sarah behind me, we made our way out into the calm waters of the Delta Rez. The oars slipped effortlessly through the water and I tried not to wiggle in my seat too much. It felt serene out in the middle—yet filled with noises from our family playing on the shore—splashing, yelling, swimming. Gratitude and love swelled within me and I thought to myself, *we will be ok*. Broken hearts mend. Grief becomes bearable, humans trudge forward through storms and sunshine. We will be ok. It will all work out.

26

You could have heard a pin drop. It was like all the air had been sucked out of the room by a vacuum, leaving only silence in its absence. A black hole swirling with disbelief. A diagnosis.

"FOSMN," [1] *the doctor explained as they stood in a circle around him. The linoleum floor gleamed in the bright lights, nurses walked by, breath was held. "Facial onset sensory and motor neuronopathy, is a very rare disease. There are only about 30 documented cases in the world. Unfortunately, we*

---

[1] https://rarediseases.info.nih.gov/diseases/

Facial onset sensory and motor neuronopathy (FOSMN) is a rare and slowly progressive motor neuron disorder. Affected people initially experience facial tingling and numbness which eventually spread to the scalp, neck, upper trunk and upper limbs. These sensory abnormalities are later followed by the onset of motor symptoms such as cramps, muscle twitches, difficulty swallowing, dysarthria, muscle weakness and atrophy. The hallmark of FOSMN is a reduced or absent corneal reflex (the reflex to blink when something touches the eye). The underlying cause is currently unknown. Most cases appear to occur sporadically in people with no family history of the condition.

don't have enough information about this disease to be able to treat it. The symptoms will slowly progress, and without treatment will leave most of your upper body paralyzed. I am sorry, but we have no cure at this time." As the doctor talked, Mom's eyes pooled with tears.

"I would like to take some pictures, and document as much as I can today so we can update our research. Would you be willing to do that, Jim?" Dad nodded and gave a thumbs up whispering, "Yes, ok". The doctor led them out of the room and down the hallway.

After five hours of waiting, Mom, Dad, Kade and the Neurologist finally emerged from behind the closed door. Sarah and Tyler looked up expectantly from the cloth covered chairs in the waiting room and met their eyes. The pale, drawn expression on Mom's face told them everything they needed to know.

"Mom, why don't we go get some lunch or something? You could use a break." Sarah offered.

"Good idea, we'll take Dad back when they are ready and text you when we are done." Tyler and Kade took Dad's arm and led him to an open seat, waving at them to go ahead. "It'll be ok, go...!"

The food sat untouched on Mom's plate. Grease from the French fries congealed as it grew cold. Her vacant eyes stared out the hospital cafeteria's window, to the street below.

I Cowboy

"Look at all those people walking around carrying on with their life as if nothing has happened and my whole world is ending."

The afternoon light faded into dusk and the grey Portland sky mirrored their gloomy mood as they left the hospital that evening. Heads hung low, defeated by an unknown disease. Tyler brought the car around to the entrance to help load the wheelchair and get Dad inside easily. As he stood up from his chair, with wobbly atrophied legs, he raised his arms up to the sky and danced around in a circle. Kade instinctively held out his arms to catch him if he fell, and Dad danced his silly dance. Laughter rang out, lifting the air—the doom they felt drifted away.

As the car left the parking lot and everyone except Dad—who refused to wear a seatbelt—was buckled in, Dad reached for his writing tablet. Head bent low, concentration painting his brow, he wrote his message loud and clear, "I Cowboy."

His determination and strength were infectious. The rest of the ride home wasn't spent in turmoil and grief, but in gratitude for finally getting an answer, knowing what they were up against, and formulating a new plan for Dad's care. "I will fight. I am a cowboy." He insisted. Everyone there that day agreed; his attitude helped them accept the inevitable. Diagnosis be damned.

27

"I feel different today. Like a huge weight has been lifted off my shoulders. I just feel different." Mom had just woken up after only a few hours of sleep. Wearing her familiar turquoise bathrobe and bare feet, we went outside to watch the sun rise and listen to the birds. "I hardly slept at all, but I feel so much better today." She said quietly and sat down across from me. It was the day after the one-year memorial—often deemed a turning point—Mom had been keeping a silent vigil within herself just trying to make it to this day.

"What do you mean?"

"I'm not sure. It's like I've reached the one-year mark and now I realize I am over it. I made it through the hardest year of my life and I feel relieved now." I took a sip of my coffee before responding. The milky warmth slipped easily down my throat.

I Cowboy

"It has been an incredibly hard year for you, Mom. I have seen you grow in many ways and I hope you know how strong you really are. It takes a lot of bravery to face what you've had to face." Clutching the coffee mug tightly between my hands, I tried to sound strong as I spoke. "I know how much you miss Dad. We all miss him so much."

"Let's watch old videos of him after you get back from your hike with Sarah. He was such a silly guy. He always made us laugh."

"Good idea. We should only be an hour or so, then I'll make breakfast. How does French toast sound?"

"Sounds delicious."

"It will all work out, Mom. Remember?"

"Yes, we got this. I Cowboy!" she said through her tears and pointed to the memorial bench I had made for her and its inscription. Two words that held so much.

The morning sounds of pots and pans, stirring and frying, eating and chatting, maple syrup and melted butter covered up the expansive hole we all had in our hearts. For now, we were ok. For now, we could go on. For now, we had each other. And then, all of us would leave and go back to our homes and families. Mom still had to live alone, sleep alone, cook alone. After fifty years of having Dad as her companion, she was on her own now. It was the first time she had ever lived by herself. After marrying right after high school graduation, she moved out of her childhood home and into a house with a new husband. By 19, she was pregnant with my oldest brother and she'd had someone by her side ever since. This was a new era for her. Life; Part Two.

The next couple of days were spent surrounded by family. We hiked and picnicked, drove through red cliff canyons to a mountain carved lake and played word games in the car. Our shared history and experiences in the past year linked us together in a beautiful, haunting way. Sitting lakeside with my brother, Robert, and finally being able to talk face to face about what had happened to Dad, healed the deepest of wounds lurking within me. When it was time to drive the 700 miles back home, I had a different perspective on loss and grief. If my Mother could climb up out of the abyss of sadness and pain, I could too. Yes, I was a Cowboy's daughter.

28

The shades were drawn, the room dark. A whirring sound from the humidifier and a voice recording of a man reading scriptures; the only sounds in the room. Dad was resting in his recliner, arms propped up by pillows. The miniature dachshund, Rudy, asleep on his lap and Dad's hand resting softly on his back. The air smelled of eucalyptus oil and the sweet tinge of sickness. I closed the front door behind me and its hinges creaked my arrival.

He looked up as I entered the small apartment. "Hi daughter," he whispered.

I forced a smile. He had gotten worse.

It had been a month since the hospital stay in Boise, and the disease had silently, unforgivingly progressed. After hearing from Sarah that he had been to the emergency room four times in the past week, and after having a terrible dream about him, I flew to Portland to see him.

A few weeks prior, after they had gotten his diagnosis from OSU, they had moved into a little two-bedroom apartment an hour outside Portland. Dad wanted to be closer to the coast, to Sarah, and her husband Devin. (He was the emergency room manager at the nearby hospital, and could routinely come and check on Dad.) They assumed the role of nurse, emotional support and constant companion for Mom. It was not an easy job—helping care for a parent seldom is—a trial of strength and character, life changing and selfless.

Kade and Tyler had made the move happen while Dad and Mom rested at Sarah's house. The boys drove back to Weiser, rented a U-Haul and enlisted the help of the church members to pack up all of their belongings, then drove the four-hour trip back to Portland. It was a colossal undertaking, one that required great determination, love, and unselfishness. Children do what they see.

It had been a harrowing week of hospital visits due to his heartrate and oxygen levels fluctuating at all hours of the day or night. The pneumonia was back. This time with a vengeance. Antibiotics by the handful and morphine tablets were the routine now; a slow-moving tsunami was overtaking him and all he had to hang onto was a life raft of faith.

I crossed the room quickly and bent down to embrace him. "Hi Daddy. How are you?"

I Cowboy

He winced. "Not so good."

I frowned and sat down on the couch next to him, trying my best to stay calm. Trying hard to pretend that I wasn't worried.

"Can I get you anything? Are you in pain?"

He nodded and closed his eye, a single tear slid down his cheek. It was the saddest moment I have ever experienced, watching defeat take its hold on him. The shadow of death was upon him. I knew our days with him were numbered. I was determined to make them count.

The ocean was a place that soothed my Dad's soul. He longed for the sound of the waves, to walk on the beach barefooted, blue Wranglers pulled up, water lapping at his ankles. This was my goal during this last visit; get him to the ocean. High tide, low tide, cloudy, rainy, or sunny. I knew it would be a stretch for him, but this was my calling. We decided on Cannon Beach, a small, serene beach town only an hour away.

I asked my little brother who was visiting at the same time to come with us. Mom was relieved. The more help we had, the better. This was our trek, a pilgrimage to the sea.

Robert offered to drive, and Dad sat up front packed in pillows with his brown beanie propped on his head. Mom, me and little Marcus, (Robert's 2-year-old son), and the dog, Rudy, squished together in the back. The car was loaded with jackets and hats, his wheelchair and medications, water and snacks for the ones who could eat them. There were homemade chocolate chip cookies, Dad's favorite. We quietly ate them while he sat in the front seat, not able to partake in the ritual. Trying to be a good sport, he said jokingly, "Where's mine?" The gooey bite sat melting in my mouth, now sour with guilt. I cringed and forced it down my throat, vowing to never again take eating for granted.

After winding our way over the tree lined, mountainous pass to the ocean and stopping to administer medication and water through Dad's tube, we found our way to the parking lot of Cannon Beach State Park. The winds were light and fresh, clouds sparse, and the roar of the waves crashing on the long, flat beach before us; a welcome sound.

People passed by with dogs and kids, shovels and buckets with well-worn blankets tucked under their arms and picnics nicely packed into bags. The air smelled of seaweed and clam chowder from the nearby restaurant perched neatly on the beach. Its outside deck was packed with tourists posing for pictures and chomping down French fries.

"Look, Jim! That's where we ate last time we were here, remember?" Mom called out from the sidewalk leading to the beach. "That was just last year..." Her voice trailed off as reality sunk in.

Sunlight streamed through wispy clouds as Dad made his way into the wheelchair. I walked ahead of the group with little Marcus, unable to accept that Dad couldn't walk the short path to the beach on his own anymore.

I Cowboy

Time stood eerily still as my youngest brother, strong and capable, pushed Dad and the wheelchair down the sandy, wet ramp. Every five feet or so Dad would insist on walking a few steps. He clung to the railing with white knobby knuckles, his knees shaking, feet unsteady, heart stubborn. After ten grueling minutes they finally reached the sand. Robert bundled him up in a blanket and heavy coat, pulled his hat down over his cotton ball stuffed ears and parked him near a rock. Mom sat nearby and held his hand.

"I'm going to miss you." Dad told her.

"I'll miss you too." She answered and kissed his cheek.

I ran after Marcus towards the ocean's edge, my feet slapping the wet hard sand. He was playful and full of joy, laughing his infectious two-year-old laugh. I couldn't help but wonder how his life would unfold. One life ending, another beginning. We all walk this path, an endless circle.

Dad sat and watched us play. His eye watering from the cold wind, a half-smile upon his face. I knew he wanted to run up behind us, grab our waist with his firm grip and pretend to throw us in like he had done so many times before. I knew he wanted to put his feet in the salty water and feel cleansed by the cold. I knew he felt trapped in a body that had ran its last race down the beach towards the oceans edge. And yet, as I walked back towards him with sand between my toes and tears in my eyes, I felt my father's love beaming from his smile. He had surrendered.

The wind blew cold down my back and I knew it was over. Our day at the beach had to end. Dad was shivering as Robert pushed him in his wheelchair back up the ramp. The sand building up in the wheels was making it almost impossible. Robert gritted his teeth, dug in his heels and pushed. The muscles in his arms strained with the weight, but he did not stop to complain or rest. He forged on as if it was not a burden at all; a child became the father and the father became the child. When they finally reached the top of the concrete ramp, Dad stood up, reached for Robert and hugged him. "Thank you," he said quietly.

As we silently drove away from the beach, headlights shining on the inky black road, sun setting in a vast open sky, I felt our hearts were finally at peace with the path laid before us.

They told us there was no cure to his illness. But they lied. There was a cure. It was called Love. Surrender. Acceptance. Family. The cure was not in the pills, or infusions, surgeries or scans. The only way out of pain is to go through it. Day by day, moment by precious moment. You will need valor, strength, and faith—as deep and pure as an immense wide ocean. In the end, that is all that matters anyway.

29

The truth is, I cry every day. I'll be walking or listening to music or just playing with the puppy, and it hits me. He's gone. I'm not sure I will ever be the same. It has been 17 months and grief has become a part of me. A giant sandbag of tears. All it takes to get the tears to flow is looking at his picture, or listening to his voice in videos saved on my phone and I'm in a puddle again, mascara smeared, eyes red, heartbroken. Over and over and over again. They say it takes years to finally accept a loved one's death. I think it takes a lifetime.

Death is a sorry, sad topic. Not many people will let you mull it over with them. Too scary. Too many feelings. Can we change the subject already? The exception; those who know the same pain. They have experienced it, they get you. Those are the ones who let you share your story—and then you listen to theirs. It's hauntingly beautiful how humans can bond over pain. I felt the same after

I had my first child. I was part of something. I had unknowingly been accepted into the Mother's Club. These willing mothers wanted to hear my birth story. They wanted to share theirs. We had an understanding. Death. Birth. It's all the same. Something we can't control and have a hard time accepting.

A few months after he died, I was walking around like a zombie, unable to put my day together into a familiar routine or pattern. I felt like I was losing my mind. A fight with my husband sent me into a tailspin and I stormed out the door into the street and screamed my bloody head off. It felt good. It felt right. It also felt like I could slip into the rabbit hole of insanity and never return. So, I started begging for help. Tears rolled down my swollen face as I marched down the street in flip flops towards the only place I knew to be of comfort. The Tamalpais Cemetery.

"I need help. I need help. I need help." I sobbed, my fists balled up, heart spilling open. An angry red blister was forming on my foot underneath the too tight strap of my cheap shoes. I didn't stop. I didn't care.

I made my way up to a quiet corner with headstones of all sizes spread out before me. The land of the dead. An orange sun was setting behind a billowy pink cloud as I lay my head down upon the dry grass and wept like I have never wept before. Sounds came out of my body that I had never heard

I Cowboy

before. I wailed and stomped my feet. I called out to the heavens, WHERE DID YOU GO?

After a while, my sobs receded. I was eerily calm as a breeze moved through the eucalyptus trees blowing cold upon my wet cheeks. It was as if the eye of a hurricane had just passed over me. Gingerly, I sat up and looked around to survey the damage. A grey- and white-haired coyote stood ten feet away, staring at me. His posture was poised. Dark and beady eyes searched mine. I held my breath for a moment wondering what he would do. Then, waved my arms and yelled as loud as I could, "Go away!" Startled, he ran down the steep road, only turning once to glance over his shoulder. I felt sorry for shouting at him. There was something about his demeanor that felt peaceful. Almost familiar. Two wild creatures meeting; the raw beauty reflected in the other.

It was dusk so I rose to leave, dusting grass and dirt from my backside. Looking behind me, I read the headstone that I had laid down and poured my tears upon. It read; PETERSEN. My family's last name.

Sometimes help comes in the most unexpected places, like the yellow Tiger Swallowtail butterfly that follows me around. It showed up weeks after he passed away, bouncing and flitting in the warm June air, free of constraints and burdens. I watched it hover around me and land in a nearby tree. It watched me. I felt a calm sense of lightness and joy overcome me as the butterfly and I exchanged our beingness. A butterfly is an evolved species. It goes through a life changing transformation in just a matter of weeks, and when it emerges with newly painted wings, it takes to its new life with courage and trust. Just like my Dad—faced with a trial bigger than himself—he found ways to bring joy and happiness to all those around him.

The butterfly is a constant in my life now. I spy it often, in my garden, on walks through my favorite woods, outside the grocery store. I stop every time the yellow and black spotted wings flit and float by. I say, "Hi Dad. Thanks for the reminder." Have Joy. It will all work out.

30

One more day with my Father; the only man who'd been a constant in my life, a towering presence of guiding light. Nothing on this big ball of green earth ever prepares you for that last day. Nothing.

After a restless night, I took my ruffled pajamas and hair to the kitchen and eagerly put together a cup of coffee. Dad was resting in his recliner with Rudy sleeping on his lap. "Morning Daddy," I said and leaned in to kiss him on the head. "How'd you sleep?"

"Not well." He whispered. "My side is hurting me." He rubbed his left side to show me.

"Is that from sleeping on the couch? Or do you think it's the infection?"

"Probably both."

"Sorry you're hurting today. After your breakfast shake let's get you outside for some fresh air. It will lift your spirits."

The back porch of their apartment was the only reprieve they had from the daily routine of medications and feeding tubes, wheelchairs and panic buttons. They loved to go sit outside and watch the trees sway in the wind, listen to the birds and say hi to neighbors walking by with dogs and kids. The simple things of life are always the most beautiful. On our walk around the building that morning, pushing Dad in his wheelchair while he scooted his legs along, we noticed other porches decorated with plants and lights, hummingbird feeders and chairs. So, I did the only sensible thing I could think of. I took Mom to Home Depot.

We loaded up our cart with flowers, containers, soil, strings of lights, a windchime and a glass hummingbird feeder. We purchased gloves, a small trowel and a watering container.

"It's too much, TiNille. I don't want you paying for all of this." Mom complained at the checkout counter.

"I'm doing this, Mom. You have to let me. It is a gift, ok?" I smiled and rubbed her back. "Besides, you love gardening. It will be so good for you. Don't worry about it, Mom. It's worth it."

Tears filled her eyes. "You always know how to help us. You always do. We are so grateful for all of you."

"It's been such a rough year for you both. You need a quiet space to rest and ponder. It's all you have right now."

That afternoon, we planted hope, we planted love, we planted dreams. As the grey rain clouds cleared and let in a little light, a patch of hopeful blue sky opened up and the sun shone brightly on our newly planted flowers. We dusted our dirty hands off, swept up the spilled soil, and announced to Dad we were done. He wheeled himself through the open door and smiled. "Job well done," he said and gave us his double thumbs up. A look of satisfaction crossed over his face as he settled into the chair and lifted his chin up towards the sky. It was as if the entire earth breathed in this moment, delivering an unseen sigh of relief for our overburdened shoulders.

The air smelled sweet with the lingering touch of rain as we made our way to a nearby park to spend some time in nature. These little outings were so important for Dad. Dressed in his plaid pearl snap button down shirt, grey sweats tucked into his shiny black cowboy boots and brown fleece beanie atop his head, which he pulled down over the sagging left side of his face, "So I don't scare anyone off."

The park was a fifty-five-acre oasis of towering trees, paths, green lush grass and a small lake. It was a perfect place to spend the few hours I had left with him.

My two sisters, Jan'l, (the eldest girl—she was staying for two weeks to help out—undeniably the hardest weeks of her life so far) and Sarah, were already there waiting for us with their kids. Sarah's oldest son, Cooper spotted us first and came bounding over to greet Grandpa. Always the playful one, Dad took the plastic bat Cooper was holding and started hitting balls out into the field for the kids to chase. Little feet ran without abandon, laughing and out of breath, willing to bring the ball back to the man they adored. Grandpa. A man they all looked up to with love and maybe a little fear. For he was also the man to douse them with a bucket of water or tease them with plastic spiders, tell them their hair would fall out like his and watch in delight as they squirmed when he milked their pigeons and gave them horse bites. Grandpa. No other man could fill his place. He was theirs. And he would travel thousands of miles to attend their baptisms, sing happy birthday or take them camping. Grandpa. A man who sat in his wheelchair with an incurable disease, pain and weakness wracking his body, and joy pumping from his failing heart to play a game of ball with his grandkids. Grandpa. A man who lived and breathed for his family.

As the afternoon waned and we had pushed his trusty wheeled horse throughout the entire park, we paused near a grove of pine trees to soak in the smell. Picking off a small branch, I rubbed the needles together, held it to my nose and took a deep breath.

"Ahhhh, reminds me of Christmas. My favorite smell." I commented. Dad waved me over to let him partake. He closed his eye, inhaled and softened his face. "Yes, smells like Christmas." His eye stayed closed, he became very still, like the surface of a pond in the early morning light, and then fell into sleep, right in the middle of his sentence. I stared in disbelief. The wrinkles in between my brow deepened as a blinding truth sunk down in the hollow of my

chest. The truth feels very heavy. An unspeakable weight of knowing. He didn't have much time.

The rest of the day was a blur with that burden of knowing. It sharpened every moment and shaped every thought. That knowing held me, opened me, rocked me as I lay my head on his chest that evening. I soaked his shirt with my tears as he rubbed my back and told me he loved me. He whispered in my ear that he knew his family needed more work. He wanted to be able to stay a bit longer, but he knew it was time. I told him I was happy and well taken care of and not to worry about me. We held on for a long time; a slow melting of unspoken fears.

I slipped into sleep, waking up at 3 am to check on him. I tiptoed out of the room and paused in the dark hallway. The glow of light from the humidifier helped guide me through the small choked room to the couch. He was propped up by pillows but his head had tilted forward. Trying not to wake him, I gently adjusted the pillow behind him. I was reminded of watching my own kids as they slept. I used to feel so vulnerable in the absolute love I felt for them. Their beauty and innocence so pure as they slept. I used to wonder what they were dreaming about, and rub their soft hair and cheeks, feeling so lucky to be their Mom. And now, as I lightly reached down and gently caressed my Father's face, I knew the truth. His life was complete.

31

Autumn is here. The trees are making their slow dance into hibernation, squirrels are busy collecting food before the rain, and fires are engulfing acres of parched, dry land. This is the driest time of the year in California, and fire season has become the norm. My neighbor's heads are turned up towards the smoky sky impatiently awaiting the arrival of winter. One can't help be attuned to nature's seasons when the signs are everywhere. With Halloween just weeks away and large orange pumpkins decorating most porches in our neighborhood, the wheel in the sky has turned once again towards change.

It is everywhere. Dried fallen leaves crunching under my feet as I walk a beloved trail, grasses that used to shimmer green in the sunlight are drained of color, and acorns litter the sidewalks now; a slow leaning of our heads upon the earth.

I Cowboy

Every living thing is part of the cycle. An endless cycle of life and death.

They don't tell you about this part. After the funeral and grieving, after the flowers you've placed near the headstone dry up; there has to be acceptance. I fought it like a toddler fights a bath at night. With every ounce of my stubborn Petersen heart, I fought it. Staring at his pictures, I would think, it can't be true. He's still here. I will see him again! I will touch his scratchy cheek and hug his bear chest. He is not gone. And then, one day you know. You accept the truth.

Acceptance is not forgetting. It is liberation from pain.

I saw it in his eyes on that last morning before I left for the Portland airport. After a long hard hug, I slowly stood up and went to the open doorway rolling my suitcase behind me. I paused and looked back at him once more. Never one to like goodbyes, he waved his hand saying, "Cheerio!" As a single tear slid down his face, I witnessed acceptance written within his brave, tired soul.

The Autumn winds signal the arrival of winter, and I walk eagerly towards it.

32

May 14, 2019

It was six-thirty am. The room was dark and the sky outside was grey with familiar fog. I pulled on a sweater to take the chill off my arms, then checked my phone for any messages. For the last two weeks, this had been my ritual. I had known this day would come.

There was a message. I read the inevitable words on the screen and my knees buckled. I reached for the cold granite counter and steeled myself to be strong.

The message was from Mom but it was sent from Dad's phone.

- *Please pray for Daddy. We are at the hospital and they just removed his oxygen. I don't think he's going to make it out this time.*

I Cowboy

Squeezing my eyes shut, I prayed to whoever was listening; please lead Dad towards the light. Take away his pain and let him be free. Just moments later, a sense of ultimate peace washed over me. I felt his spirit close as I crossed the dark room to sit in my favorite spot; a brown leather, well- loved recliner that faced the backyard windows. I watched the birds fly from branch to branch, their morning routine; a reassurance. I breathed. I waited.

My heart beat quickened and I typed my last message to him, although I knew he would never read it— I love you, Papa. Patience, I told myself. A few minutes later, anxiety overwhelmed me so I called my sister to get an update. It went straight to voicemail. I waited. I breathed. The birds danced upon first lights' branch.

After a very long hour, Sarah finally called back and filled me in on the prognosis.

"Dad took off the C-Pap breathing machine and said, Enough! The nurses had to comply, and so did we. I told him I loved him," She paused as tears choked her voice. "He said he loved me, told the nurses thank you, and gave them a thumbs up. He hasn't opened his eyes since then."

I told her I wanted to talk to him, and she had me wait while the nurses left the room. Before holding the phone to his ear, she said with a hushed voice," He is slipping fast, but I know he can still hear us. He is ready to cross the river, Sis. It's his time."

TiNille Petersen

The words spilled and tumbled out of my soul; words only spoken on the threshold of death. With shaky cold hands, I said goodbye to the man who had always led me, guided me and loved me. I can't remember what I said, it has blurred into a space saved just for us, but I knew he heard me; I felt his love straight through the phone. I pictured him in the hospital surrounded by love, by light, by family. I envisioned him getting on his horse, and crossing that river. Go Dad! Be free of this body. You will be alright. Your family is near and you will be guided home; back to the place we all came from. I will see you there.

It wasn't much longer and he did just that. His broken and frail body released the magnificent soul that he is and finally; set it free.

He rode his trusty horse across his wide, wide river and paused. Looking back, he tipped his familiar brown Stetson, looked at his family waving from the other side, love beaming from our eyes, and steadily, proudly, rode into the light.

33

Grief is a lonely state. It holds one hostage within an empty shell and only briefly will let you go. In order to go on living in a world that's always in a hurry, one finds small respites of time that its ok to be ok. One realizes that grief will have its way—it becomes an old friend—will you invite it in for tea and really listen or send it away?

If you are living, then you have probably experienced a loss of some kind. When you are a child, this is hard to understand. I remember losing a beloved puppy. His name was Joey and he was very spunky. I adored him. It was just a few short weeks later that Joey died suddenly from Parvo. I was devastated. Even at ten years old I understood the finality of death. We gathered in the backyard and dug a shallow grave. Shovelfuls of dirt piled on top of his little brown and white body and I cried silent tears for the friend I was just getting to know. I'll never forget the purple scented lilacs I picked and placed neatly on top, and the misshapen rocks we lined the grave with.

There is a story of a woman who lost her only child. She was inconsolable, alone, living in grief. She went to the Buddha and asked him to help her heal—and if he couldn't, she would refuse to go on living. She would follow her child to the grave. Karma or no karma, she would not live this way. The Buddha agreed to help her but first told the woman she had to bring back a mustard seed from a home that had never known any sorrow.

And so, the bereft mother set out to look for one. Her search was arduous. She went from city to city, house to house, all over the world. She could not find one that had not known grief or sorrow—but, she was shown many other gifts—for every house knew her pain and wanted to help ease her journey. When the woman returned, she showed the Buddha what she had been given: strength, tenderness, acceptance, courage, compassion, empathy, love and wisdom. "I didn't find the mustard seed, but I was given many other things." She told him.

"How do you feel now?" He asked.

"Different. Each gift has comforted me in so many ways. My heart has been enlarged to carry them all. What is this full, heavy feeling?"

"Sorrow."

"I am like the others now."

"Yes," whispered the Buddha. "You are no longer alone."

34

Delta, Utah. Land of sagebrush, farmers and windstorms. Home of the infamous Topaz Mountain, endless miles of bright white salt flats, rattlesnakes and sunsets that lasted for hours. A wide sky dotted by stars and the International Power Plant smoke stacks blinking their lights: red, white, red white. Delta. The land of my birth. A place we called home. Wide swaths of land cut in patterns by one lane roads. Signposts and irrigation canals used for directions. Men wearing tight blue Wranglers decorated by oversized belt buckles of silver and gold, behind the wheel of a beat-up Ford with a mangy dog by his side. A land of prayers. Mormon pioneers settled here despite the dry caked earth, hardened by years of drought. They stayed anyway and dusted their hands off, getting to work. These people are my tribe, my roots, my family; we are "Deltan's". Many years have passed since I laid eyes on the large wooden triangle sign marking the outskirts of town, "Welcome to Delta. Settled 1907." The last time I was in this small forgotten place, I was still a naïve girl with a freckled nose who thought her Papa would live forever.

The A-team was back together and our long journey was almost over. Mom, Sarah and I flew from Portland to Las Vegas and drove six hours to finally reach the two- lane highway into Delta. We ate Cheetos and red licorice, Dad's favorite road trip snacks. Many tears spilled from our dark circled eyes and the holes in our hearts felt unfillable. The lumps in our throats; a permanent fixture.

Dad was already there. He was transported on a special flight and we would meet him at the Delta Funeral Home. In the three days prior, we had to make several hard decisions, write the obituary and plan most of the services. The last decision would be the hardest we would ever have to make. As we walked around the funeral home, holding hands, our hearts breaking thousands of times over, and looked at coffin after coffin, I couldn't help but wonder where they were keeping him. I fought the urge to run away and fling open the many closed doors hoping to find his body there.

The coffin we chose was made of pine and had images of evergreen trees wood burned into the lid. We all agreed it was the best one. I cringed imagining him laying inside of it and held back oceans of tears so I could help Mom sign the papers. Amber arrived and gave me a worried look. Mom's voice had risen to an unnatural pitch and she was fidgeting with her purse straps. I rubbed her back to try and calm her. She looked at me with wide, vacant eyes, "I'm fine! I really am!"

The amount of the funeral services and his coffin were added up. We all gasped at the total. $11,146.00. The date of his birth. I knew it was a sign. Smiling at the significance, we all felt it. He was still with us.

The next morning, the rest of the siblings and their families trickled in from their travels. One from Alaska, two from Hawaii, two from California. We had to meet the caretaker later that afternoon so it was decided we would spend the morning visiting the ancestors— starting with my Mother's parents. It was a day of driving through our pasts, remembering where we had come from, honoring those who'd gone before. The soul remembers what the body wants to forget. And as we toured our homeland, I couldn't help but think of death as a beginning.

The weather mirrored our moods. The high desert winds gusted through tree branches. Raindrops spotted the dry concrete, painting the dust with polka dots. A storm hovered over Delta and forced us to button up our coats and cover our heads. No one slept the night before. A war-torn shell-shocked crew arrived at the cemetery to do the unthinkable; pick out our Father's plot.

TiNille Petersen

I slammed the car door and started out across the grassy field to where the caretaker stood. Bits of wet grass stuck to my shoes and ankles as I weaved my way around the many headstones. I paused to read a few. Reid. Petersen. Anderson. More ancestors here. This land was brimming with their stories, sweat and tears. It was Dad's request to be buried here in the form of a letter found in the metal safety deposit box they kept all their treasured and important papers. On the front of the envelope was written, in Dad's flowing cursive, Myrna. "I didn't even know it was there. He must have written that recently." Mom explained. Inside, were his last wishes. I looked around at the peaceful, quiet grounds and knew why he had chosen this place. An Oasis in the desert, hard to get to, easy to forget. Surrounded by flat rolling land that met the mountains with ease. One could breathe here, one could rest.

All eight children gathered around Mom as a ray of sunlight burst through the thick, ominous clouds. Its light shimmered and sailed through the rain-soaked air, casting a glow on the grass below our feet. The ancestors wrapped their loving presence around our tribe; we were a family at peace.

Delta. The land of my birth. The place we will lay my Papa to rest. Life is a circle. An endless circle.

35

I knitted a red hat and gave it to my Dad for Christmas a few years ago, and now it is back in my care. Mom returned it to me along with all the cards and letters I had sent him over the years. I held his worn hat against my nose for a long time breathing in his scent. I could still smell him woven into the fabric. I never imagined I would be holding his hat again. I never imagined it would mean so much.

Knit, purl, knit, purl. One stitch at a time, weaving together the fabric of our lives. Each stitch represents a time, a story, a minute, in the huge span we call our lifetime. There may be gaps. Backward stitches. Slipped stitches. Knots. These "mistakes", I realized, are not mistakes at all. These are bumps, bruises and obstacles along the way where I learned a thing or two; don't hold the yarn too tight, keep count or you'll lose your place. These lessons in the stitch are visible only to me.

As I show my finished piece to someone, they only see a hat, or a scarf.

What can be learned by the slow steady pace of knitting together a life?

- It takes time, but it's worth the work.
- This involves many long, arduous hours of repeating the same pattern over and over.
- You have to be willing to do the work.

Knitting together the fabric of our life's work into a recognizable pattern is painful, and slow going. Sometimes you are nearing the end of your piece and you realize you have been putting the wrong pattern together. Knitting instead of Purling. It is at these turning points that you have to make a crucial decision. Continue? Or unravel the whole thing, stitch by stitch and start again. This time you knit in a different way. You cast on and begin, continuing one stitch at a time. This time with more awareness. You are paying attention now. This time you will get it right, because now you realize the thread was spun long ago, by the oldest cause of all—your soul.

Knit, Purl, Knit, Purl. A slow unraveling took place for all of us while we witnessed what nature had prescribed for our Father to bear. His willingness to "do the work", proved to all of us that we are never given more than we can handle. He embraced the pain. Even if he didn't want to. He learned from it. And in the end, he gave thanks for it. For it had shown him who he really was; a man who was capable of enduring and overcoming any obstacle.

Illness had given him a way to knit together a new fabric for his life. One that was not filled with regret and heartache, self-hate or doubt. He knitted over past mistakes with love, forgiveness and understanding; making them whole. He showed us all that even through life's greatest challenges—we would overcome. Now, his work is complete. It's our turn. We get to do the work now.

EPILOGUE

Keep in mind how fast things pass by and are gone—those that are now, and those to come. Existence flows past us like a river: the "what" is in constant flux, the "why" has a thousand variations. Nothing is stable, not even what's right here. The infinity of past and future gapes before us—a chasm whose depths we cannot see.
–Marcus Aurelius, A.D. 121-179

Humans are like little rivers in constant motion and evolution. Some are like a roaring, raging river. And some are a slow trickle of water moving down a warm, sun baked canyon. In time, we all go back to the same place; just as every river leads to the ocean. Our lives; a vast open body of water that changes and flows. Everything is unknown, yet familiar. Each human, each river, each wave, big or small, is a part. All beings play a part in this ever-flowing existence.

I often think back on the day I sat by the Snake River as my Father lay in a hospital bed, just mere blocks away, attached to IV's and tubes, riddled with pain and pumped full of antibiotics. I think of the cold rock I sat upon watching the dark water flow by and the grief I felt watching him suffer.

The river told me a story that day. A tale so ancient I already knew the words, and still do. Go with the flow, it seemed to say. We can't stop the flow of life; it is constantly changing.

This past year has brought many changes and heartache to our family and yet, we remain. We will ebb and we will flow, just like a river. One thing I know for sure; the lessons I learned from a Cowboy.

–Try to be a little bit better every day. Be kind. Laugh. Tease someone. Dance. Pray. Gaze at sunsets. Enjoy life; don't let it pass you by. Cherish your family. Help a neighbor. Charity. Humility. Faith. And most importantly; when life seems unbearable and you want to give up, DON'T. Keep fighting for what you love. Saddle up, hold your head high and ride.

I Cowboy.

In loving memory of James Wallace Petersen
January 11, 1946- May 14, 2019
Happy Trails to you, until we meet again....

AUTHOR'S NOTE

Writing this book was incredibly cathartic for me. It was a labor of love from start to finish, and I hope I have been true to the story as I experienced it. All memoirs are subject to the perspective of the author. I had to change a few scenes for the flow of the book to make sense, and some of the events I was not actually present, but tried to envision the scene using my imagination and other family members memories.

The sharing of our stories is what truly completes us as humans. We learn from each other and from our experiences. After all, it is the journey, not the destination that counts. We exist; for each other. As the unfolding of this book materialized after my Father passed away, the lessons of my life as his daughter and the story of his passing overwhelmed me. I found it very hard to continue writing at certain points; I was having to relive all the pain once more. But—in the telling, I found strength, healing and a new found zest for life. That is the truest gift that writing has given me.

I was at an incredibly low point towards the middle of this book. I was stuck. The inspiration to go on was alluding me until I heard something on the radio that changed my entire perspective. The radio host was recounting a story of Mozart. He had just published a few of his recent compositions and was receiving some backlash from critics and editors. When asked how he felt about the criticism, Mozart replied," I am writing for hearts, not publishers."

My hope in writing this book is to not only inspire others to live their best lives despite their circumstances but to educate people about the commonly misunderstood and overlooked symptoms of the very rare disease my father suffered from. FOSMN is a slow progressing and debilitating disease. Shining a light upon any darkness helps to diffuse it. That is my goal. By sharing this story, I wish to bring other families suffering like he did, some light.

More information about FOSMN can be found here: https://fosmn.org/

A day in the park
Double thumbs up!

Tini Thank Love my #1
PAPA giRL
go Take care of your Thank you
So much for your Insights and
the Falcon

Home?

I don't Like goodbye

I Like Hellos

Wedding day—August 21, 1970

Ocean Beach, Oregon—2018
RV Adventures

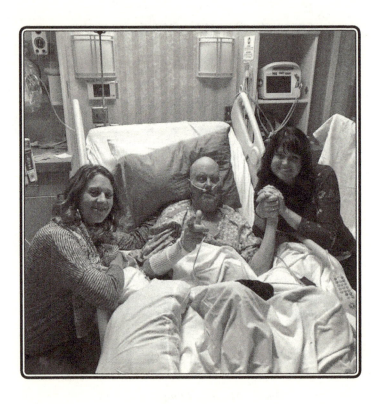

The A-team

The Petersen Tribe
Kade, Justin, Myrna, Jim, Jan'l, TiNille
Amber, Robert, Tyler, Sarah
Circa- 1994

ACKNOWLEDGMENTS

Dad—WE did it! Thank you for helping me remember, and for being such an incredible Papa. I will miss you every day of my life, and love you for thousands more. Your legacy lives on and it's a beautiful one.

Mom—You are an inspiration. Your bravery and strength are remarkable. I am so proud to be your daughter. This book is for you.

Petersen Tribe—You mean the world to me, thank you for your love and support.

Angeleah, Ana, Tracy, Alyssa, Romi—True friends are hard to find. I am so blessed to have found you. Thank you for your truth, support and authenticity.

Sherry and Tim—I am honored to be your daughter…you have taught me so much and accepted me from Day One. Thank you.

Jason, Makenzie, Delaney, Sherwood—My true roots and foundation begin with you. You make me what I am and give my life incredible meaning. I love you with all my heart.

Sarah—my A-team partner and fellow Go to Girl—thank you isn't enough for all you have helped me with. Our lives will be forever entwined in a beautiful way. Thank you for always being one I can depend on.

I Cowboy

Made in the USA
Las Vegas, NV
22 June 2021